3 THINGS
KIDS NEED THE
MOST

Other books by Fred A. Hartley III

Dare to Be Different
Dare to Date Different
Flops: Turn Your Wipeouts into Winners
Update: A New Approach to Christian Dating
Growing Pains: First Aid for Teenagers
What's Right, What's Wrong in an Upside-Down World
The Teenage Book of Manners, Please!
*Men and Marriage: What It Really Means to Keep That
  Promise*

3 THINGS KIDS NEED THE MOST

Parenting At Its Best

Fred A. Hartley III

SPIRE

© 2003 by Fred A. Hartley III

Published by Revell
a division of Baker Publishing Group
P.O. Box 6287, Grand Rapids, MI 49516-6287
www.revellbooks.com

Spire edition published 2009

ISBN 978-0-8007-8736-3

Previously published by Revell in 2003 as *Parenting at its Best*

Printed in the United States of America

To my associate Jack Bruce and his wife Julie, who exemplify much of what is contained in the following pages as they parent their four children, Amber, Seth, Lydia, and Anna. On the wall of Jack's office hangs this inspiring note, handwritten by his son Seth:

"Special Memories"
One day last year we went to the beach in Florida.
We stayed there three days.
On the last day it was very early in the morning.
My dad and I went fishing at the pier.
And we fished a long time.

I caught 21 fish. My dad caught 31 fish.
And then we ate lunch together.

We went back to the hotel.
We had a great time talking.
I think that is a special memory.
I had a chance to be with my dad.
11-16-2000

Contents

Foreword

Our son grew up in the sixties, when life and values were changing very rapidly. You want to talk about a parenting challenge! We learned a great deal about faith in those days, and we accomplished far more on our knees than by shaking an accusing finger.

In the fall of his senior year of high school, Fred suffered a severe concussion from a football injury. Following preliminary tests, the doctors told us how seriously his brain was bruised. We could fret and worry over his situation, or we could give him to God and ask for healing. We gave him over to God. While God does not always choose to heal, he did in this case. God touched Fred and miraculously healed him; this became a turning point in his life.

We are grateful to be able to say that our son lives what he writes about. His family celebrates the great adventure of life. Years ago we dedicated him to God, and he is now using his gifts and talents to serve many. We are confident that this book will help you tap into parenting at its best!

Al and Hermine Hartley

Preface

For twenty-five years I have respectfully turned down the invitation to write a parenting book. Who am I to give advice—and on such a personal subject? I decided to leave it to the experts.

Well, I am still no expert and I maintain a high regard for the individuality of parenting styles and the uniqueness of each child's needs. In writing this book, I remain a fellow student with much to learn about raising children. I often feel like Indiana Jones in one of my favorite movies, *Raiders of the Lost Ark*. When asked, "What are we going to do now?" he replied, "How do I know? I'm making it up as we go along!" As a parent, I have often felt like that.

What qualifies me to write about parenting? Quite frankly, I still ask myself that question. There are several realities, however, that have made this book possible:

- My wife, Sherry, is a great mom, and I've had a front-row seat to observe her character and her parenting techniques.

- Each of my four children has been very patient with me. They love me and have taught me tons.
- My parents continue to leave fingerprints of blessing on my life.
- I have enjoyed a special relationship with all four of my grandparents.
- Since we were first married, Sherry and I have observed effective parenting and we have both read extensively on the subject.
- I am a faith person. Through my intimate relationship with God, I have learned vital principles on how to raise children with a passion for life.

Parents, you shoulder enough pressure, challenges, and guilt. You don't need me adding to your stress. My goal is to bring you courage, dignity, and honor on every page. That is my commitment to you. If you don't feel a little lighter, a little more confident, and a lot more excited about parenting when you have finished reading, I have not done my job. And, if all goes well, this book will become a dog-eared soul mate, like an old pair of jeans or a trusted friend, as you navigate your way through the fearful yet wonderful parenting years.

Introduction

Help! My Kids Need New Parents

They are a generation stuck on fast forward, in a fear-some hurry to grow up. Richer than ever, they're also a retailer's dream, with a seemingly insatiable desire for the latest in everything. What should parents do?

Newsweek, October 18, 1999

In the concrete world full of souls
The angels play on their horn all day,
The whole earth in progress seems to pass by.
But does anyone hear the music they play?
Does anyone even try?

Bob Dylan

We were standing toe-to-toe, decked out in our rented tux-edos, my firstborn and I. It was his wedding day—T-minus two minutes and counting. In a rare backstage moment, prior

13

to the wedding, we locked eyeballs and gazed into reservoirs of memories overlapping three decades. I thought about all the miles we had put on our tires; the countless Little League games, beach trips, belching contests, late-night pizzas, and late-night talks; all the funny, awkward, tender, formational, teachable moments. It didn't seem like too long ago that I had stood in the delivery room wearing blue jeans and a T-shirt for our first father-son bonding moment, gazing with wonder for the first time into those steel-blue eyes.

We reached out and wrapped our arms around each other in an effort to hang on to that moment and make it last a little longer. I slapped his back, "You da man, Fred!"

"No, Dad," he replied, once again looking deep into my eyes and deeper into my life. "You da man. You're the best man!"

Those words triggered a rare rush of dignity that pulsated through my masculine soul and caused every cell in my body to tingle. It was magical, spiritual, fulfilling. My firstborn could not have made me feel richer if he had handed me a check for a million dollars. At his request I was officially serving as his best man. What an honor to stand at his elbow as he stood on the threshold of the rest of his life! But when he looked into my eyes and at point-blank range fired the words, "No, Dad . . . You're the best man," he hit a bull's-eye, touching a big, soft spot somewhere deep inside my chest cavity. He was not simply referring to my formal role in his wedding; he was affirming my mentoring role in his life.

Parents long to stick their straws into moments like this and suck for all they're worth. And why shouldn't we? Parenting is supposed to be fulfilling, isn't it? The moment we gaze for the first time into our child's eyeballs, we get a taste of the nobility, the honor, the dignity of parenting. This is one of only a few genuinely awe-filled events in life, feasting our eyes on our newborn daughter or son. This moment is more majestic, more glorious, and more awe-inspiring than any seascape, sunset, or mountain range we will ever glimpse. Just the sight makes us feel richer. It is at the same time both wonderfully invigorating and overwhelmingly terrifying. The magnetism of this moment draws us, yet at times its weighty responsibility makes us want to run and hide. We instantly recognize the sobriety of the sacred trust we have received as a dad or mom. So much is at stake. Our child's eyes become full-length mirrors, providing us with a look into our own souls that is deeper than any X-ray machine or MRI. The reflection we see of ourselves in our children is so indescribably enchanting, so juicy, so fulfilling, so succulent, so addictive that we never again want to live without it.

There is just one problem. Many of us have not taken a swig from that jug of parenting fulfillment for a long time. Somewhere along our child-raising journey, the awe, the majesty, and the dignity of parenting got buried under the burp cloths, dirty diapers, detention notices, and speeding tickets. Some of us are so parched right now that our lips are cracked and our tongues are sticking to the roofs of our mouths. As Dr. Jay Kesler, former president of Taylor University, has said, "Young people have always had growing pains, but today the problems are often deeper, more intense, and more complex."

Simplify Parenting, Please!

Parenting has become much too complex. Most of us tend to yank our children in too many diverse, and at times conflicting, directions. We want to be good parents and at times we try too hard. We are well aware that our children have needs, and we feel the primary weight of responsibility to meet those needs, investing enormous amounts of time, energy, and resources trying to do so. Just take a deep breath and think of a few of the needs we frenetically try to meet in our children's lives: academic, athletic, financial, musical, social, intellectual, psychological, recreational, cultural, artistic, moral, ethical, extracurricular, interpersonal, career, emotional, marital, religious, sexual, and spiritual. *Gasp!* It is little wonder our kids feel pulled in too many directions.

One parent said to me recently, "My child is on two soccer teams, the track team, plays trombone in the school band, and sings in the church choir. We feel as though we've exchanged childhood for a treadmill!"

As we will see in the following pages, being good parents is less complex than we think. For our own self-evaluation, let's take a survey. From the following list of needs in your child's life, which would you identify as the most time- and energy-demanding right now? Put a 1 to the left of the need of your child into which you put the most time and energy. Now put a 2 next to the second-most time- and energy-consuming need of your child. Do this for the top five.

___academic___	___extracurricular ___	___psychological___
___artistic___	___ financial___	___recreational___
___athletic___	___ intellectual ___	___religious___
___career___	___ interpersonal ___	___sexual___
___cultural___	___ marital ___	___social___
___emotional___	___ moral ___	___spiritual___
___ethical___	___ musical___	

Having indicated where you currently invest the majority of your time and energy resources, it might be helpful for you to go back through the same list, placing the same five numbers on the right side of the corresponding need indicating where you think you *should* be investing your resources in your child's life. To which needs would you say you should devote the greater time and energy, according to their importance to your own value system?

No doubt each of the above needs is important. It could be argued that some are even highly important. In the pages that follow, however, you will discover that none of them represent your child's essential, core needs, those which are chiseled into the wall of every single cell in your child's body, ingrained into his psyche like his genome. We will identify the three fundamental needs in your child's life. We will learn not only how to recognize these needs but also how to meet them. We will discover that though these needs are obvious, they are often overlooked. And we will learn that the reason for so much parental unfulfillment is that many parents have failed to identify the three basic needs of their children. Our children know instinctively something is missing, yet they cannot put their finger on it. We as parents know instinctively something is wrong, yet we can't find the handle.

I Want Something

A Stanford University student returned to her Malibu Beach home over spring break and locked herself in her bedroom; she cried for three days. Her parents knocked, appealed, and tried in vain to get an answer. "Honey, what's wrong?" Silence.

"We have given you everything." Still no answer.

"We have sent you to the finest university. You have plenty of friends. You have good grades. You have a brand new car. What is it? What else can we give you?"

Finally, their daughter yelled in desperation, "I want something, but I don't know what it is!" More hard tears followed. Then silence.

Many families face silence, no solid answer, confusion, and few returns on all the time and energy investments. It is sad how much parenting comes up empty. It is all too easy to feel like a parenting failure. A mom stings from rejection. A daughter's words can cut so deeply. A son's anger can pierce like a saline syringe. A frustrated father, who can run a multimillion-dollar company that turns a handsome profit, has a son who won't even talk with him and a daughter who mocks him. Fathering and mothering promise the moon and yet all too often deliver bumps and bruises.

Now, let me clarify. All the needs listed previously are real and worth meeting. We would be shabby parents not to look after these needs in the lives of our sons and daughters. However, there are three essential core needs that all our children have, and these are even more important. It is possible to meet all other needs in our child's life and yet miss these three. It is impossible, on the other hand, to meet these three needs without also meeting most of the other needs at the same time. It is a matter of priority and a matter of essence. The area of greatest need in your child's life is reflected from his or her inner being, and that is where we want to give our highest priority. Chances are your child will never walk up to you, tap you on the shoulder, and say, "I appreciate the great education, the trust fund, the athletic training, the music lessons, but when will you begin meeting my deeper needs?" That is not going to happen. But don't let that fool you. In this book you will discover how relevant these three heart cries are to your child's growth and maturity and to the effectiveness of your parenting. Beyond the more superficial needs, down where too few parents dare to journey, are the three fundamental, strategic core needs that deserve our undivided attention. These three needs can be stated very simply.

The need for acceptance

The need for affection

The need for affirmation

It doesn't matter how young or old, how slow or quick, how outgoing or reclusive, how right-brained or left-brained, how motivated or unmotivated, how East Coast, West Coast, or Heartland, how rap, punk, R&B, easy listening, or heavy metal—from crib to casket, your child is silently (or not-so-silently) craving these three blessings. And they are blessings. Your child is looking principally to you to meet these three core needs. From her belly button to her button nose, she wants to hear you express to her acceptance, affection, and affirmation. More than protein and carbohydrates, he hungers for fulfillment of these three needs.

This book is structured in three sections, one section for each of the core needs inside the belly of your child. My goal is to give plenty of practical insights into not only how to recognize these three needs but, more importantly, how to meet them. And, yes, you will receive plenty of encouragement for your own parental soul along the way.

The Three Basic Needs

Let's just take a sneak peak at these three inner needs.

The need for acceptance growls from the pit of your child's belly. She desperately wants to know her distinct identity, her design, her self-worth. Whether she verbalizes it or not, she is constantly asking the question, "Am I okay? Am I normal? Am I any good?" Or beyond that on a deeper level, "Am I worthy? Am I worthy to be a daughter? Do I make the grade?" Bottom line, "Am I accepted?" More specifically, "Do *you* accept me?"

Chapters 2, 3, and 4 will equip us to answer these questions and to communicate acceptance effectively.

The need for affection is often more awkwardly expressed. Children do not always feel comfortable showing affection, much less asking for it. It may sound clumsy, fumbling. It probes a child's relationship potential, friendship potential, family life and intimacy potential. The need for acceptance has to do with your child's self-worth, independent from others; the need for affection, on the other hand, has to do with his worth in relationship to others. This goes far beyond the superficial "What do they think of me?" and at the deepest level asks the questions, "Am I likeable? Am I friend-worthy?" The acceptance need asks the question, "Am I worthy to be a son?" But the affection need asks, "Am I worthy to be *your* son? Am I worthy to be your friend? Am I likeable?" The need deep down begs to know, "Am I loved?" And more personally, "Am I loved by you?" Chapters 5, 6, 7, and 8 will empower us to pour into our child the affection he or she is craving.

The third inner craving of a child is her *need for affirmation*. It has to do with the effectiveness, success, and fulfillment of your child's potential. The first two needs deal with the child's being; this third need deals with the child's doing. Your child has an assignment, a task, a responsibility, and her need for affirmation gives her continuous internal evaluation. Somewhere beyond the tattoos and loud music, your child is begging to know, "Am I effective, productive, competent? Am I achieving anything of worth?" All children are inwardly longing to know they are reaching their potential, that they have what it takes. No matter how they define success, they want to know it is achievable. Chapters 9, 10, and 11 will give us the reserves we need to shower our children with healthy and life-giving affirmation.

When you combine these three needs, they determine your child's sense of well-being more than any other factors. As we saw with the California college student who cried, "I want something, but I don't know what it is," it is possible for all your child's needs except these three to be met and yet he or she still feel empty. These three heart cries—for acceptance, affection, and affirmation—are the essential longings of all humanity.

Perhaps the three basic needs still sound abstract to you—elusive, vague, touchy-feely, difficult to get a handle on. Let me introduce you to a word picture that may be helpful. Imagine reading your child's inner life like the dashboard of your car. We all know how to check the instrument panel and read the gauges showing fluid levels and battery charge. We are well aware that when a light comes on, we must respond quickly. Similarly we can learn how to read the instrument panel of our child's inner life. Rather than fuel, oil, and battery charge, we will be looking at the gauges that reveal his or her acceptance levels, affection tank, and affirmation gauge. We need to understand that buried under the hood of our child's life are three large, invisible, yet essential tanks to which the gauges correspond. Our child is intuitively and continuously monitoring these tanks and is all too keenly aware of how full they are. When the tanks are brimming over, life is good. When they are running on fumes, life can be hell. And it is at least partially our responsibility as parents to monitor the gauges and help to keep our child's tanks full.

Let me risk the danger of overusing a pretty good illustration and add that if our child does not feel our unconditional acceptance, he will run out of gas. If our child doesn't feel our positive affection, she will run hot under the hood, whether or not we see the engine light come on. And if our child's affirmation battery is not consistently recharged, he will lose speed in a hurry. It will not be a matter of being unable to accelerate and burn rubber. Our child will lose the spark. His engine will misfire. Or it may not turn over at all.

On the other hand, there is nothing in the world as exciting, invigorating, or fulfilling as watching one of my children hit on all cylinders. Forget NASCAR. When my kid knows she is accepted, loved, and affirmed—when her tanks are full— life is good.

What Every Child Longs to Hear

The three honest, inner longings of every child are encapsulated in a single sentence—three brief thoughts, only thirteen words. The words are simple, straightforward, and direct. In fact they are so simple, they may even sound trite, but don't kid yourself. These words are profound, refreshing, and life-giving. They represent the fuel in your child's tank, the oil in his engine, the charge in the batteries of his inner life. Every soul that has ever lived thirsts for them. Down deep, under the hood of his inner life, every child longs to hear these words. It's time we get to know them so that we can use them to raise our children's sense of well-being to acceptable levels. Each of us will express them differently. We will learn to put them in our own words. More important, beyond words, we will learn how to translate them into a wide range of actions. The key is that we learn to express them frequently and effectively and in ways our children understand.

No matter how familiar these words may sound, read them carefully right now as if your child's life depended on them. In a sense it does.

You are my son (or daughter); I love you; I am so pleased with you.

If you are a faith person, perhaps you recognize the words. They were originally spoken by Father God to his Son. When Jesus faced certain threshold moments in his life, Father God carefully utilized these identical words. Just think of it. God had every imaginable word at his command. He could have shaped any sentence or paragraph. He could have written a book or composed a lyric. But the Father knew what his Son needed. He knew about all the challenges his Son would encounter that would drain and deplete him. He had his eye on the gauges of his Son's inner life and knew how to fill his tanks.

With toes curled over the threshold of his life of public service, prior to forty days of intense God-seeking, Jesus faced his first major defining moment. He chose to demonstrate his voluntary life of obedience by being immersed in water, sort of a rite of initiation into public service. Jesus did it to obey his Dad. This single step of obedience was an acknowledgment of his submission to his life's calling, one others might not understand. In fact the record indicates others did not understand. Ultimately, however, the other voices didn't concern Jesus, for he could withstand a little ridicule. He wanted only to hear his Dad's voice of affirmation, and the Father wanted to say something that would fill the most important tanks in his Son's inner life.

With Jesus' hair dripping Jordan River water and with his face set like a flint to fulfill his life's calling, we overhear the Father whispering these three phrases to his Son—a simple sentence, thirteen words: "You are my Son, whom I love; with you I am well pleased" (Mark 1:11). This moment was so significant in Jesus' life that all four Gospel writers record it (see also Matt. 3:13–17; Luke 3:21–22; John 1:32–34). Is it not reasonable to suggest that since God the Father carefully selected these words when addressing his Son, they may well contain vital information to us all regarding the basic inner needs of our children?

It shouldn't surprise us that each of these three phrases used by Father God directly corresponds to the three fundamental inner needs of every child:

The need for acceptance—"You are my son (or daughter)."

The need for affection—"I love you."

The need for affirmation—"I am so pleased with you."

When I first discovered this connection I got goose bumps. I knew I was on to something significant, something that would benefit my wife and me as parents. If Jesus needed to hear these words, perhaps my children do too. In each of the three sections of the book, we will glean parenting insights from the significance of these phrases in Jesus' life.

There is another time that we overhear the Father's gentle voice speaking virtually these same words to his Son, near the midway point of Jesus' career. He has already been mentoring his twelve students into an effective management team. He has cast evil spirits from dysfunctional people, miraculously fed thousands, healed an innumerable assortment of physical illnesses, taught the masses, and achieved a remarkable level of notoriety as a spiritual leader. Yet what did he get for all his efforts? Anger, rejection, and a lot of bad press. In addition, he knew he was yet to face the most critical threshold moment of his life, his cruel death by crucifixion. What did the Son need to hear from the Father at a moment like this? The Father knew. He said, "This is my Son, whom I love. Listen to him!" (Mark 9:7). It should not surprise us that the Father speaks these words to refuel his Son's tanks.

"This is my Son"—acceptance

"Whom I love"—affection

"Listen to him"—affirmation (He is worth listening to)

One of the men who had a front-row seat to overhear this conversation was Jesus' close colleague Peter. This raw fisherman must have sharpened his pencil when he observed the refreshing effect the Father's words had on Jesus. This spectacular moment made such an overwhelming, lifelong impression on him, he refers to it extensively toward the end of his life when writing his second New Testament book.

> We did not follow cleverly invented stories when we told you about the power and coming of our Lord Jesus Christ, but we were eyewitnesses of his majesty. For he received honor and glory from God the Father when the voice came to him from the Majestic Glory, saying, "This is my Son, whom I love; with him I am well pleased." We ourselves heard this voice that came from heaven when we were with him on the sacred mountain.
>
> 2 Peter 1:16–18

Did you notice that when Peter describes the impact of the Father's words on Jesus, he said, "He received honor and glory . . . when the voice came to him"? This means that there was something visibly different in Jesus' countenance after hearing his Dad's words of acceptance, affection, and affirmation. Remember, this report is coming from Peter, not Jesus. In a sense he is saying Jesus was juiced by his Father's words. In short, those words from the Father filled his tanks.

Isn't that what we all desire for our children? Don't we want to fill our children's tanks by the things we say and do? And isn't it reasonable to suggest that these words from

God the Father to God the Son were so well chosen that they represent the essence of what our children are longing to hear from us? After all, these words are not just randomly selected from a long list of words spoken by the Father to the Son; they are the *only* words on record that the Father spoke to the Son. When Jesus heard these three phrases, he was on "the sacred mountain," as Peter describes it. My children need sacred mountain moments. And so do yours. Our children need moments when they hear their parents' voices bringing similarly invigorating messages.

Parenting Passion

Deposited deep inside every parent—deeper than the desire to make money, to have sex, to gain influence—is the desire to parent well. We want to outlive ourselves, generate, reproduce, invest ourselves in those we love most, and leave behind a good name—a legacy. Some will enjoy the satisfaction of seeing their name on a building, a monument, a Hall of Fame plaque, or a big, fat financial portfolio. But somehow we all know down in the basement of our souls that our names belong on more than material objects. We have a desire to invest ourselves in other significant people, to bring to maturity those we love most. This is what we call *parenting*.

So how are you feeling about your parenting?

If you were raring to go when you brought your baby home from the hospital, but now eight years later you feel like you've run out of gas—

If you feel like a parenting failure—

If you're scared to death to parent a teenager—

If parenting isn't fun anymore—

If you want to move beyond the frustrations of ineffective parenting and find the fulfillment that comes from
investing yourself in your son or daughter—

Then you qualify; this book is for you!

Parenting is much more than the weight room where a person pays his dues; it is the stadium where we face our greatest
challenges and where we receive life's highest rewards. You
may currently feel like a parenting failure. Your children may
be so alienated from you, the thought of parenting well seems
like an unreachable star. Perhaps your child is grown and
gone and you're not even sure you are still on her Christmas
card list. Your child may be an adolescent and perhaps your
home life resembles World War III. Possibly your son is a
preschooler and you're not yet able to even reason with him.
Or you may not even have biological children but are pain-
fully aware that there are children who are looking to you as
a role model. Don't even think about leaving the stadium. We
have all logged a few losses on the parenting playing field,
but that's all right. Look at it as a scrimmage; you can still
win the game.

In the name of diligent parenting, we can all too easily place
our child on the treadmill of unrealistic expectations. Rather
than enriching our child's life, we can unintentionally drain
her spirit dry. Rather than juicing our son on extracurricular
activities, we may be sapping his energy with too many interests. Our children are being pulled in too many directions
and sometimes we are the ones to blame. It's time to blow the
whistle, call time out, and simplify our lives. In the following
pages we will distill our parenting duties down to only three,
which focus on the three fundamental needs in the lives of
our children. And we will simplify the lives of our children
in the process.

For all you single moms and dads who have more gum than you can chew and who still manage to have a little energy left over at the end of the day to pour into your kids' lives, you don't need someone condemning you for not doing more. Instead, for all the pats on the back you have never received, this book's for you. I hope you will find it to be a source of encouragement, a friend, a soul mate. It may even set you free from stacks and stacks of unrealistic expectations. One thing for sure, it will help you do a few important things for a few of the most important people in your life. And it will help you do them well.

In case you have ever grabbed your hair in your hands, yanked hard, and cried, "Help! My kids need new parents!" I have some really good news: You are the parent your children desperately desire. And you alone have the stuff to fill their tanks. The purpose of this book is to help you learn how to not only read your child's gauges but also learn some tangible ways to keep his or her tanks full. There is no escaping it. As parents, our well-being is hot-wired to our child's well-being. When his or her tanks are full, we share in the overflow. When our child's tanks are low, we too will feel the drain.

For all parents who long to stick their straws down deep into parenting fulfillment, your lips may be cracked, your tongue stuck to the roof of your mouth, but there is hope. For all who are thirsting for parental dignity, this book's for you!

Like a window letting in natural light, a story from one of my four children will appear in every chapter. All the following chapters will begin with a story. In this introduction, I have saved the best for last.

A Window into My Child's Heart

The summer before my sophomore year in high school, Dad and I traveled to Boulder for our first Promise Keepers men's conference in the Colorado State Buffalos stadium.

As we drove, surrounded by the Colorado Rockies, I began thinking about my future and feeling confused and fearful. Where would I attend college and what vocation would I pursue? As I was looking over the peak of adolescence and moving toward many major decisions, I needed some serious advice concerning my personal destiny. Almost like he was reading my mind, Dad suggested I open the Bible to the Book of Proverbs. He directed my attention to Proverbs 1:7: "The fear of the Lord is the beginning of knowledge, but fools despise wisdom and discipline."

How did he know what I was thinking and what I needed? It wasn't even so much what he said. What sticks out is that he cared. He took time. He thought about me. We had fun. We talked. There we were cruisin' along, and my earthly father was encouraging me to pursue a tight relationship with my heavenly Father. What an amazing concept!

I read the next two verses, "Listen, my son, to your father's instruction and do not forsake your mother's teaching. They will be a garland to grace your head and a chain to adorn your neck." As I read this passage, I realized the importance of parenting. That afternoon, in the front seat of our rental car, I was determined to place all of my worries and fears concerning my future at the feet of Jesus. It was a breakthrough moment in my life, and my dad was there with me.

As I rewind the video of my upbringing through childhood and adolescence, I can see the obvious hand of God on my life. Throughout my years growing up, my dad has been my best friend, and he has shown me that a busy schedule can be managed in a way that would never take away from spending priority time with his children.

Fred A. Hartley IV, age twenty-five

PART 1

Meeting Their Need for Acceptance

You Are My Child

Acceptance. It doesn't sound like much. That is why it is easily overlooked. But don't be fooled—it is the number one heart cry of youth. Every preschool child is longing for it. Almost every adolescent doubts its existence. And all too many parents take it for granted.

"What is the big deal about acceptance?" a parent asks. "I'm the father. He has my last name. We share the same address. Isn't that acceptance?"

When Father God told Jesus, "You are my Son," there was a reason. Jesus hadn't forgotten this fact. He knew it in his head. But he needed to hear it again. He needed to feel it. He needed those words spoken in the voice he respected most—the voice of his Father.

"You are my daughter." "You are my son." These are words every child longs to hear. They affirm a child's unique identity. They are words of worth, dignity, honor, respect, virtue, wholeness, balance, and truth. The extent to which you learn to communicate acceptance to your child is the extent to which you will be able to effectively shape his self-esteem and build his self-worth. Each of the following three chapters will help you effectively demonstrate to your child that in your eyes she is good.

A Window into My Child's Heart: Acceptance

Hey Dad!

Last weekend with you at the Masters [golf tournament] was the best! Thanks for taking a day and a half off to be with me. It was a special time I will never forget. I was just reflecting on some of the great things that you and I have done together over the years, and the list goes on and on. Now, as I grow older and those times get shorter and less frequent, I find myself soaking up every minute when we're together. Thanks for being such a great dad! The Masters has always been a great golf tournament, but now it means even more because we were able to experience it together.

I love you!

Fred IV

1

I Accept You

The American family is unraveling like a cheap sweater. May I remind you of one historic fact: No nation has ever survived the disintegration of its home life. Once the home goes, it's just a question of time before it all goes.

Dr. Howard Hendricks

No man is an island, entire of itself; every man is a piece of the continent, a part of the main.

John Donne

It is a frightening moment when you stare at your child and silently reflect, *You are my flesh and blood; your DNA reflects mine; we live at the same zip code; we have the same address, phone number, and last name; and yet for all practical purposes you and I have nothing in common.*

A well-known marriage book, *Men Are from Mars, Women Are from Venus*, suggests the radical differences between the sexes. There are times our own child seems to be from Neptune or Pluto. We don't speak his language, and he surely doesn't speak ours. Our differences range from our interest in music, radio stations, and weekend activities to clothing, facial hair, tattoos, earrings, body studs, and how to spend spare time. At times there is an apparent Grand Canyon of differences that separates us. Have you ever stood on the edge of the Grand Canyon? I have. I stood on the north rim, got in my rental van, and drove toward the south rim. Six hours later I got out of my vehicle and looked back.

Imagine standing on the south rim, attempting to parent a child on the north rim. Believe it or not, that is precisely how I felt ten years ago toward my firstborn. He and I share the same name, only I am the III and he is the IV. Obviously we have the same gender. And we have similar mannerisms. Yet from my perspective we had virtually nothing of substance in common. I'm a charger; he's laid back. I was more task-oriented; he was more people-oriented. I loved exercise; he was your classic couch potato. I was spiritually demonstrative; he was spiritually reserved. There was probably a love for God way down deep, but on the surface I couldn't even get his spiritual pulse. I can remember a road trip we took together. We sat eighteen inches apart, yet despite some of my finest efforts, I could elicit no more than a grunt or two and maybe a dozen words in three hundred and fifty miles. It was painful.

This is the same son who nine years later would ask me to be his best man. This is the same son with whom I walked the Masters and who wrote me the letter that opened this chapter, the same son who now calls me his best friend.

What changed? How did it happen? Quite simply, we found common ground. Better than that, we learned to celebrate common ground. But it didn't come naturally. As we dig into this life-giving parental insight, we will open our *Sports Illustrated* and look at the life of Bo Jackson.

Bo Knows Parenting

Bo Jackson was the first world-class athlete to play two professional sports—baseball and football. For the Kansas City Royals in 1989, he hit thirty-two homeruns, drove in one hundred and five runs, and was named MVP of the All-Star Game. He was the first Major League Baseball player to shag fly balls with his bare hand during a game and, after striking out, break the bat over his knee or even on occasion over his helmet like it was made out of balsa. Then ten days later, after the close of the baseball season, he joined the L.A. Raiders and rushed 950 yards in only eleven NFL games. The next season he was picked for the Pro-Bowl.

Even after his career-ending hip injury in 1991, he loved to crisscross the country, making public appearances for a big fat profit and filming unforgettable Nike ads. He loved driving his Harley Davidson, Viper, and Mercedes. He quickly became known as Mr. Bo-Knows-Baseball and Bo-Knows-Football and Bo-Knows-Soccer and Bo-Knows-Everything. Or so we thought.

In October 1995 the front cover of *Sports Illustrated* featured a handsome mug shot of Bo Jackson and asked an intriguing question: "Not long ago Bo Jackson was the most famous man in America. Then he disappeared. What became of Bo?"[1]

Even if you're not a sports fan, you might identify with Bo's definition of a father:

My own father, do you know what I thought a father was? A man who came to your house every month and a half and left a $20 on the table. . . . My father has never seen me play professional baseball or football. I tried to have a relationship with him, gave him my number, said, "Dad, call me. I'll fly you in." Can you imagine? I'm Bo Jackson, one of the so-called premier athletes in the country, and I'm sitting in the locker room and envying every one of my teammates whose dad would come in and talk, have a beer with them after the game. I never experienced that.[2]

Can you hear what Bo is saying? All the screaming fans in the stadium couldn't satisfy his need for acceptance; he wanted it from his dad. Even with all the camaraderie he had with his teammates in the locker room, his need for affection was unmet; his heart ached for his dad's affection. But he and his dad couldn't find common ground. And even the multimillion-dollar paychecks from Nike couldn't satisfy Bo's need for affirmation; deep down he longed for his father's blessing. There was a wound in his soul, a void inside. But Bo was smart enough to make an effort to give his children what he never received from his father. "Whenever I had free time, I spent the whole day with my kids." He insisted on being a hands-on dad. "My children will be loved," he vehemently promised his wife Lynda.[3]

His efforts, however, didn't seem to carry the ball across the goal line to score a touchdown with his kids. His look-alike son, Nick, innocently asked his mom in his dad's absence, "Why is Daddy never home? Does he have another home with more kids?" Those words were like a beanball that smacked Bo upside the head, tearing his baseball helmet permanently off. When he picked himself off the dirt and dusted himself off, he immediately announced his retirement. Suddenly Bo woke up to realize a parenting principle some of us have yet to learn: Our kids aren't impressed with our free time; they want our priority time. During priority time and extended time, we discover common ground.

That day Bo Jackson called his agent and his sponsors and told them he quit. No more heavy travel, no more extended trips, no more absentee dad. He wanted his kids to have what he never had—a dad who cared, a father who was there, a father who listened, who laughed, who appropriately touched. In a sense, he retired young to give his kids a full-time dad.

I can almost hear someone saying, *Well, sure, who wouldn't want to retire young, with your garage full of hot cars and a fat bankroll, and spend all your time with your kids? But that doesn't look like my zip code.*

No, obviously not everyone can quit his or her job, but we can change our focus. Remember, Bo learned that his kids needed priority time, not just spare time. You can be sure your child can sniff out your motivations a mile away. Your child knows what makes your eyes light up. She knows what makes your head turn and your heart beat faster. Your children want to know they are part of the action, not where you turn when the action is over.

We all know that Bo knows baseball and Bo knows football, but it is also nice to know that Bo knows parenting. When it came right down to it, his kids never felt the adrenaline rush of the screaming stadiums. Come to think of it, neither did Bo. His fast cars were fun but unfulfilling. Even the sports posters that hung on thousands of other kids' walls were not what his children wanted. All they wanted was a daddy whose name happened to be Bo Jackson, with whom they could spend some time, hang out, play. Fortunately for them, Bo is learning what it takes to find some common ground.

Common Ground

Common ground, quite simply, includes anything we share in common that is big enough to support a relationship. It includes common interest, common activity, common schedule, common language, and common heart.

In the world of business, common ground is the room to negotiate the deal. In international relations, common ground is the point at which two independent sovereign nations can maneuver toward a peaceful treaty. In a court of law, *grounds* is the term for legal standing—the right to bring an argument, to plead your cause. In computers, common ground is the language in which a computer thinks and communicates with other computers. And in the vast world of parenting, common ground is the place where both the child and the parent can communicate in a common language, and both can walk away understanding what was said, feeling connected in a healthy common relationship.

Needless to say, lacking common ground can be highly irritating, frustrating, and nerve-racking. Our tendency is to think, *I shouldn't have to hunt for common ground. This should be a given. My kid needs to get it through her thick skull. I'm the boss-parent; she is the subservient kid. End of story.* For 10 to 15 percent of all children, this may work. If that's the case for you, consider yourself fortunate and skim through to the next chapter. For the other 85 to 90 percent, you will be glad to know there are some very helpful steps you can take to begin drawing your daughter or son back alongside.

Discovering common ground is essential to effective parenting. It enables us to communicate with, shape, motivate, impact, affect, and connect with our child. Without common ground, our words fall on deaf ears. Our advice goes unheeded. Our finest efforts are for naught. Sound familiar? Fortunately there is help.

Listening

It is easy to think the tongue is the most important parenting tool in the body. With it we give advice, correction, and counsel. With it we can encourage, admonish, exhort, warn, even scold. No doubt about it, the tongue is an important parenting tool. But if we're considering the *most* important tool in the body, I want to make a case for the ears. Even in sheer numbers, the ears have the tongue beat two to one.

Listening is becoming a lost art. Even the Bible wisely advises, "Everyone [including parents] should be quick to listen, slow to speak and slow to become angry" (James 1:19).

If there were a Listeners Hall of Fame, I would nominate my own dad. Growing up in the sixties and seventies, I presented many challenges to him including domestic, lifestyle, political, moral, spiritual, and financial issues. He was a World War II veteran, having piloted a B-17 bomber all over Europe. I filed as a conscientious objector. He was into big band and swing music; I preferred Bob Dylan, Santana, and the Moody Blues. He was a Builder; I was a Boomer. He was establishment; I was antiestablishment. He was conservative Republican since his father had been a U.S. Representative and cosponsor of the Taft-Hartley Act. I was progressive Independent. He was pro-military; I was anti-Vietnam. He was middle class value system; I wasn't. He was short hair; I was long hair—really long. He enjoyed shaving; I liked whiskers. For him punctuality was a core value, for me a source of irritation. He leaned toward controlling; I leaned toward free spirit. Add it all up and you have a Grand Canyon of distance between us.

He could have easily squished me like a grape. His wing tips could have stepped on me in anger and no one would have noticed. Instead, my dad took me to school, enrolling me in Listening 101. He became the world's greatest question-asker. He drew me out and created a safe place for me to spill my guts and express my opinions and my feelings no matter how off-the-wall they were. He would come into my room, put on my stereo earphones, open the album jacket, listen to my music, read the lyrics, and then discuss the philosophy of my favorite musicians and songwriters. Looking back, I realize it was his ability to listen that earned him the right to speak into my life. He did more to shape my worldview and my philosophy of life through our late-night discussions of the Doors, the Who, the Rolling Stones, the Beatles, the band Blood, Sweat and Tears, and Dylan music than all the semesters I had in high school.

I can remember spending time in friends' homes and overhearing their parents scream, "Turn down that noise!" or "Turn off that trash!" and thinking, *Wow! I never hear that harsh, demeaning tone in my home. My dad's awesome!*

Listening says, *I respect you and I value what you're thinking. I respect your perspective. I want to give you the gift of a listening ear and I want to give you the gift of time. We don't need to rush. I care about what you think. Your viewpoint is important to me. I accept you for who you are. You always have something of value to say. I like to hear your voice. You are one of my favorite people. You are worth whatever time it takes for us to understand each other. I am a better person when the thought patterns from your brain shape the thought patterns in my brain. I may not agree with you, but I respect the logical process your mind is taking. I communicate dignity to you. I don't want to speak out of ignorance before I listen. I don't want to prejudge. You may be right. While our tastes are different and our preferred styles may vary, I want to understand where you are coming from.*

Each of these statements represents realities we want to emphatically communicate to our children. Punch all that into an adding machine and, bottom line, it equals acceptance. All that and more is communicated every time we stop to listen. What an important parenting tool the ear is!

Listening takes time. As Richard Swenson, author of the classic book *Margin,* told me as we sat in my office, "Personal listening requires unhurried leisure. Leisure is a quality of spirit, not a quality of time. When I'm too busy, schedule too crowded, I'm not free to listen. If I provide margins in my day, there is ample time to listen."

Along with the ear, the eye is an important parenting tool, handy to use to communicate acceptance. In fact, the ear and the eye share much in common. Unlike the tongue, which tries to alter the surroundings, the eye and ear are simply agents of acceptance. They both take in information. The ear receives audible stimuli and the eye visual. In evaluating our child, particularly when, despite our best efforts, our child remains largely nonverbal, the eye can be a most helpful tool.

What Will You Give Your Boy?

What is the gift you give your boy?
A glamorous game, a tinseled toy,
A whittling knife, a puzzle pack,
A train that runs on a curving track?
A Boy Scout book, a real live pet;
No, there's plenty of time for such as that.
Give him a day for his very own
Just your boy and his dad, alone.
A walk in the woods, a game in the park,
A fishing trip from dawn to dark;
Give him the gift that only you can
The companionship of his "old man."
Games are outgrown and toys decay
But he'll never forget if you give him a day!

Author Unknown

Be Smart

Every parent of a teenager might as well get used to the idea that we are shock absorbers. It might be in fine print, but it's in our job description. I promise. There is nothing flattering about calling ourselves shock absorbers. It's not pretty, but it is functional and honest.

Teenage tongues don't intend to be cruel or mean-spirited; at times, however, it just comes naturally. The teenager's hostile expressions don't so much reflect his feelings about you as his feelings about himself. A large part of what junior and senior high students verbalize is spoken under the unofficial heading, "Tell me it isn't so." Many heated arguments between teenagers and parents are an indirect way for the kids to say, *I really don't believe these things, but I've been thinking about them, I hear them at school, and I don't know where else to go with them. So would you give me your feedback?*

The commonsense proverb "A gentle answer turns away wrath" (Prov. 15:1) must have been written with parents of teens in mind. "A gentle answer" is another term for shock absorber. When your adolescent comes at you with hormones raging and attitude on the edge, you have a choice. You can be smart or stupid. You have the right to power up, pull rank, show 'em who's boss, give her a piece of your mind, get more angry than she does, raise your voice to a higher decibel, and crush her like a grape. You can if you want to, but that would be stupid. On the other hand, you can be smart. You can listen, ask questions, draw her out, and let her express her feelings, even her anger or her ignorance. Give her the gifts of patience, kindness, reason, respect, honor, care, and sensibility. The choice is yours. You decide.

Stupid	Smart
Yell	Listen
Give answers	Ask questions
Talk louder	Talk softer
Frown	Smile
Demand respect	Give respect
Be angry	Be gentle
Express insensitivity	Show sensitivity
Be irrational	Be rational
Be undignified	Be dignified
Be proud	Be humble
Show disrespect	Be respectful
Control	Empower
Exhibit a "case closed" attitude	Be open to reason

Part of the price tag of listening is that it takes time. This is both the benefit of listening and the bother. It forces us to slow down, process, think, communicate, and respond. But the result is common ground.

Good Questions

If listening is an essential skill for effective parenting, good questions are the tools of the trade. We should know this. When our child gets sick, we take him or her to the doctor and we listen to the doctor's key questions: "How do you feel? Where does it hurt? How long has it bothered you?" From the moment the doctor or the nurse says, "Open your mouth. Say, 'Ahh,'" till the time we pay the bill, they are asking questions—good questions.

Why do we think it is any different for all the other growing-up challenges our child faces? There are constant general maintenance needs for which our child will require proper diagnoses, and there are special issues that will surface from time to time. We don't have to have a degree in psychology to learn how to ask effective questions. All we need are sincere love and respect for our child and a willingness to come alongside in the pursuit of his or her best interests.

Good questions come alongside. They communicate respect, trust, and dignity. Good questions are an arm of friendship that offers encouragement and support. When you listen to a person ask well-crafted questions, it is a thing of beauty. It's like watching Tiger Woods swing the club or Michael Jordan take it to the hoop. While some of us will never slam-dunk a basketball or clink a hole in one, we can each learn to ask good questions. I am confident we are all tired of after-school grunts and one-word answers at the dinner table. Part of the problem may be the bland questions we ask. We parents may be tired of the same old answers we get from our children each day, but what do we expect if we ask the same old questions?

Try some of the following questions for a change.

Creative School-Day Questions

Which class is your biggest challenge? Why?

Which teacher do you like best? Why?

What words would your friends use to describe you to their parents?

Has anyone ever treated you mean at school? A little mean? How did it happen? How did it feel? How did you respond?

Have you ever gotten in a fight at school? Verbal fight? When? What happened? How did you feel?

Have you ever felt rejection at school? When? How did it feel?

In what ways do your values differ from those of your friends? How are they the same?

Have any of your friends at school stood up for their convictions even when other classmates may have mocked or ridiculed them? How did you feel toward them at the time? Have you ever been in that position?

Have you ever been in a situation that required you to stand alone? When? How did you feel?

Have you ever been in a situation where you felt pressure to compromise your convictions?

Creative Weekend Questions

On a scale of 1 to 10, how stressed out and tired are you as you go into the weekend? (1 = free as a bird; 10 = ready for ICU)

Fill in the following blanks:

This weekend I'd like to _____.

The one person I can tell anything to is _____.

If I had a real problem, the one person I'd go to is _____.

When I'm hurting, the place I like to go is _____.

If I could spend one day with anyone in the world, it would be _____.

If I could spend one day with anyone in history, it would be _____.

Creative Holiday Questions

What animal do you see yourself as? Why?

What animal do you see me as? Why?

What animal do you see Mom (Dad) as? Why?

The thing I like most about our family is _____.

The thing I'd like to change about our family is _____.

The one piece of advice I'd like to give Dad (Mom) is _____.

Dad's (Mom's) greatest skills that benefit our family are _____.

The thing I admire most about Mom (Dad) is _____.

The thing I admire most about my sister (brother) is _____.

Creative Mealtime Questions

Ask only one of the following per mealtime and maybe only one per week.

If you could travel anywhere in the world, where would you like to travel and why?

If we as a family won a hundred-million-dollar Powerball lottery, what should we do with the money? (And let's say we would only get it if we could all agree on how we'd spend or invest it.)

If we could take a three-week, all-expense-paid, anywhere vacation, how would you like to spend the time?

If we as a family could solve one world problem, which would you like to solve?

If you knew you could succeed at any one thing—you could not fail—what would it be?

My favorite meal is _____.

My favorite movie is _____. Why?

My favorite book is _____. Why?

My best friend is _____. Why?

When I graduate from high school, the quality I'd most like to be remembered for is _____.

Listening to Music Questions

What in this song do you identify with?

How does listening to this song make you feel?

Why is this music enjoyable to you?

What frame of mind was the songwriter in when he or she wrote it?

Is there a message to the song, a meaning? What does it mean to you?

Do you agree with the meaning, philosophy, or perspective of the song?

Do you mind if I express to you how this music affects me?

Heart Questions

Has anyone at school ever called you a name? What was it? How did it make you feel?

What has been the happiest moment in your life? One of the happiest? The most recent happy moment?

What has been the saddest moment in your life? One of the saddest? The most recent sad moment?

What dream or aspiration do you have for your life? What one goal would you like to accomplish? What about in high school? College?

Have you ever been bitter? Really angry? Have you ever gone to bed angry? Awakened angry? Angry enough to swear under your breath? What happened? How did you respond?

Have you ever attempted something that you were afraid would not succeed? What was it? How did it turn out?

Some of these questions may sound contrived. They are not. They all work, but they need to be used under the right conditions. They are like a box of hand-tied trout flies. They can all catch fish, but you need to select the right bait for just the right situation. You know your child better than me— better than anyone, for that matter. No one can toss in a line and reel in your child as well as you. But be smart. We spell that S-M-A-R-T.

S — Sensitive
M — Mature
A — Alert
R — Responsive
T — Trusting

There is another style of parenting. We spell it S-T-U-P-I-D.

S — Selfish
T — Thickheaded
U — Unreasonable
P — Petty
I — Inflexible
D — Defensive

Building on Common Ground

In the following chapters we will learn to build a healthy relationship on our common ground. We will learn to use this ground to communicate to our son or daughter our acceptance, affection, and affirmation. In a sense, everything else grows out of common ground. To look at it another way, without establishing solid common ground, we have no basis on which to build a relationship. For this reason, I am reluctant to leave this topic prematurely. We must first be sure we have a good footing right here.

Once we ask the appropriate question, like throwing the right fly in the trout stream, and we get our son or daughter to bite, we want relationally to reel him or her in. We want to draw our child alongside, listening attentively and intuitively to what he is saying and to what he is not saying. Sensitive listening has been described as rubbing our fingers across the cracks in another person's soul. We are not trying to win favor, win an argument, or even win a friendship. At this point we are only trying to find common ground.

What can we find in common that is big enough to support a relationship? When I looked at my son and came to the painful, threatening, intimidating (dare I say humiliating?) realization that we shared virtually nothing in common, I panicked. I didn't know where to turn. I prayed, "Lord, help! Where can I begin to build a relationship? I need common ground. Where can I find it?" You won't believe the answer. As a rather structured, make-the-most-of-every-moment type of guy, guess where I initially found common ground with my firstborn? I thought for sure it would be in one of my areas of strength or interest—tennis, running, fishing. Take your pick. Not even close. I found common ground, of all places, in front of the TV set, watching weekend sports.

This did not play at all to my strengths. He knew more batting averages than I did. He knew stats of individual players whose names I didn't even recognize. But I didn't mind asking, and he didn't seem to mind answering. The most important thing was that we were talking and we were discovering common ground.

Sometimes I am a slow learner, but it didn't take me long to realize my son's favorite sport was golf. For me, watching a golf tournament was like watching paint dry or watching grass grow, but it held Fred in rapt attention. If I wanted to develop common ground, I would watch with him. I think he enjoyed teaching me, pointing out the fine points of the game. My ignorance seemed at times to entertain him. While it would violate a family value to actually wage money bets, we would guess the winner of tournaments. When on vacation and asked what he wanted to do, Fred would request an afternoon of golf. Eventually I determined that if this was going to become a viable family activity, I needed to become at least mediocre, so I took lessons. I realize that, because of all the golfing pastors jokes out there, what I am about to tell you may seem like a half-truth at best, but I can humbly say those lessons were not for me. They were for Fred. They were for common ground. Admittedly, they helped my golf game, but more than that, they helped my relationship with my son.

Last week I drove from Atlanta to Columbia, South Carolina, to play a late-afternoon round of golf with Fred before spending the next day with him walking the Masters. While riding eighteen holes, we talked about his life goals, his future career, his marriage, his finances, his recent surgery, his diet and physical fitness, his final semester of grad school, the sale of his mobile home, his savings account (what there is of it), the job application and interview process, negotiating a salary and benefits package, and a few too-personal-to-mention-in-a-book items. I would say that is an extensive relational superstructure built on the common ground of TV and golf.

The day of Fred's wedding, I paid for all the guys in his wedding party to play a round of golf. Fifteen greens fees.

Ouch! I took care of the tab, but Fred took care of pairing up the foursomes. After all, Fred plays with his two brothers and me regularly. With all his buddies converging from all over the country, surely he'd want to get next to some of them. I was eager to hear with whom I'd be playing. *Probably Fred's future father-in-law. Maybe my brother-in-law or an old friend,* I thought. And Fred's partners? Which of his buddies would he be playing with? When I asked him, I couldn't believe it. As I write these words at this moment eighteen months later, I still tear up. He chose to play with his two brothers and me. "Who else would I play with?" was Fred's response. "That's not even a question." That is more than common ground; that's common roots. That's loyalty. That's depth of relationship. It was even worth fifteen greens fees.

Your Common Ground

Common ground can be found while rebuilding an automobile, doing yard work, cliff climbing, camping, hiking, cooking, scuba diving, traveling, shopping, reading together or discussing favorite books, working on computers, or doing household projects. Just about any healthy hobby will work—music, art, dance, intellectual pursuits, athletic or recreational activities. And the more talk time, the better.

Those of us with several children know that each child occupies his or her own space, and therefore we are required to find common ground with each of them. With some it will come naturally and with some it will be like searching for sunken treasure. But the treasure is there. And it is most certainly worth the search.

One final reminder. As you scour the landscape for a piece of real estate you and your child can call common ground, don't expect it to be necessarily in an area of your strength or your interest. It may very well end up in an area of your weakness, even an area of disinterest. So what? It's not about you (or me). It's about your child. You want to meet your child on her ground. You want to claim the ground with her. You want to move into it like Marco Polo, Magellan, or Christopher Columbus, charting new territory with your child. You might as well get used to it. Good parenting requires the spirit of adventure.

The best parenting doesn't take place until we accept the fact that our children are far more than extensions of ourselves. Each one is his own unique, autonomous person. Our children have ground they will occupy that extends way beyond anywhere we have ever been. When we discover this, it should not be intimidating but rather motivating, compelling, invigorating. We can't regard the search for common ground as an infringement on our convenience. Rather, it is an opportunity for our own further advancement and for meeting our child's need for acceptance. We are accepting her for who she uniquely is—not a projection of ourselves—and enjoying the revelation of her distinct self. Once we discover and then celebrate our child's uniqueness and her distinct interests, we gain tremendous influence to effectively meet her need for acceptance.

To return to the cover question of *Sports Illustrated*: "What Became of Bo?" Why did he hang up his cleats, forfeit a multimillion-dollar ad campaign, and say good-bye to a world-class career and world-class notoriety? To put it simply, he laid it all aside because he wanted to stand in his driveway around three o'clock every afternoon and watch his kids get off the school bus. Common ground with his kids was worth more than all the airtime and media coverage.

One heartwarming footnote to this story is that Bo Jackson has also reconnected with his dad. Following a hip rehabilitation session in Birmingham, Alabama, he drove to the small town of Raymond and looked up his father. "We sat down, had a talk, and I told him the things that had been eating me up." Only two weeks before the *Sports Illustrated* article was written, Bo was working on some hunting arrows at his workbench in the basement and the phone rang. It was his dad. "Sitting in this chair, right here. First time he ever called. Took him thirty-two years to realize he had a son that loved him."[4] Now Bo knows parenting and Bo knows blessing. He is gaining fulfillment from both generational sides of life.

In the next chapter we will see how to build on the common ground once it is established. Before you turn the page, ask yourself these tough questions:

With my son or daughter, what can I honestly call common ground?

Do we have an openhearted, I-can-say-anything-to-you and you-can-say-anything-to-me relationship?

In review, which of the questions in this chapter might be just the trout fly I need to toss into the stream of my son's or daughter's life?

What in my life might I need to lay aside (like Bo Jackson) to discover common ground with my son or daughter?

A Window into My Child's Heart:
Understanding

Dear Mom and Dad,

I've been thinking about some very important lessons learned on the playing field—of athletics but also of the game of life. I was the only senior on the team in my fourth year of playing varsity basketball, and I thought I would easily be the top player. But my confidence was quickly deflated when my coach told me that she considered me the number five player on the team that year.

When I came home that day, Dad said, "Your coach should be ashamed of herself!" That made me laugh, but I also remember his following words of motivation and encouragement. Every day at practice I worked harder, ran faster, and gave extra effort in everything to show that I wanted to win more than my teammates—and it worked! What could have been a quitting point turned out to be a new beginning.

That experience taught me that what other people think is not as important as the words of the Lord.

You have helped me learn this by always being on my side, cheering me on as my biggest fans. You were always there for all my games, making sacrifices to watch even those pitiful middle school early-morning Saturday games. You have always supported me and helped me have a positive yet balanced perspective on my abilities and potential as a ballplayer and even more as a person. Most important, you have both done your part to build character in my life by not trying to solve my problems for me; you gave me godly advice and encouraged me to make my own decisions and talk out my problems with those involved.

In all of my endeavors, you, Mom and Dad, have provided me with the confidence and daily assurance of your love by always being there to watch, cheer, encourage, applaud, and challenge me to become a better person. For all of these things and more, I thank you.

All my love,
Your one and only daughter—

Andrea Hartley, age twenty-three

2

I Understand You

I've got two kids who were really easy to raise and two kids who were a real challenge.

Chuck Swindoll

Sometimes our desire for simple solutions prevents us from seeing problems clearly.

Howard Hendricks

The only thing worse than the day in a parent's life when he or she looks in the face of his or her child and silently reflects, *Who are you?* and *How did you get this way?* is the day in the child's life when he looks in the mirror and says something similar about himself.

In the last chapter we learned how to respond as parents when we face the gnawing question, "Who is this child and from whom did he or she get this?" We learned how to establish common ground with our daughter or son on which to build a meaningful relationship. Now we want to discover how to be a help and not a hindrance to them when they face their identity formation.

The term *identity crisis* is much too strong to describe the experience of most young people. *Identity formation*, on the other hand, is an essential part of every child's maturation process and is not something to be dreaded. We should welcome it and utilize it for maximum mutual benefit. In one way or another every child comes out of the womb screaming, "Who am I? Am I okay? Would someone please tell me!" They obviously don't verbalize it, at least not right away. But sooner or later they will, and that's why parents are there. Perhaps there is no more significant role for parents to fulfill than to intentionally and explicitly reflect back to their child an accurate, honest, encouraging view of who he or she is.

Winston Churchill's Dad

By all outward appearances, when he was growing up, Winston Churchill had everything a boy could want—wealth, privileges, servants, education—all that accompanies aristocratic status. He was the Kennedy or Bush of his generation. However, under the surface there was a hollow cavity. Servants and orderlies raised him, and, at the earliest possible age, he was sent off to boarding school. His interaction with his world-famous father, Lord Randolph Churchill, was sporadic. It is reported that he never ate with his parents until he was a teen and even then only on rare occasions.

As a young man, Winston was thrilled when he was accepted into Sandhurst Military College. Although a public school and not the same as his dad's alma mater, a private cavalry school known as the Sixtieth Rifles, it was nonetheless prestigious and quite an honorable accomplishment for young Winston. He eagerly awaited his father's favor. On hearing the news, Lord Randolph sent his son the following letter:

[You should be ashamed of] your slovenly, happy-go-lucky, harum-scarum style of work. . . . Never have I received a really good report of your conduct from any headmaster or tutor. . . . Always behind, incessant complaints of a total want of application to your work. . . . You have failed to get into the 60th Rifles, the finest regiment in the army. . . . You have imposed on me an extra charge of some 200 pounds a year. . . . Do not think that I am going to take the trouble of writing you long letters after every failure you commit and undergo. . . . I no longer attach the slightest weight to anything you may say. . . . If you cannot prevent yourself from leading the idle, useless, unprofitable life you have had during your school days, . . . you will become a mere social wastrel, one of hundreds of public school failures, and you will degenerate into a shabby, unhappy and futile existence. . . . You will have to bear all the blame for such misfortunes. . . . Your mother sends her love.[1]

No approval. No acceptance. No affection. No affirmation. No value. Instead, a wound. Renowned historian William Manchester, in his biographical classic *The Last Lion*, says, regarding the death of Winston's father, "It is clear now that Randolph, had he lived, would have been a crushing burden for Winston's parliamentary ambitions."[2] In other words, the best thing his father did for him was die—a sad commentary. Make no mistake, Winston went on to greatness, achieving honors that surpassed his dad's, becoming prime minister of England and being knighted by Queen Elizabeth.

Something, however, was still missing. Who doesn't hunger for approval? Who doesn't yearn for acceptance? Who doesn't need affection and affirmation? Who doesn't long to be valued, to be treated as more than an old, neglected VCR, lying on a discount table at Wal-Mart, selling for bargain basement prices?

Everyone experiences identity formation. It is the grid through which we evaluate ourselves and by which we determine our self-worth. The process of identity formation takes place largely during the years of childhood through adolescence. From then on, our identity becomes the basis by which we measure our significance for the rest of our lives. We can be highly successful by many other standards, but the only standard that matters to us is the one inside our own soul. Sir Winston Churchill was vastly successful according to virtually every standard outside himself, but the one standard that perhaps mattered to him the most was not so kind.

The following poem is written from a son's perspective, but it certainly applies equally well to daughters.

Daddy, Do you Want Your Boy to Be Like You?

> There are little eyes upon you, and they're
>   watching night and day;
> There are little ears that quickly take in every
>   word you say;
> There are little hands all eager to do anything
>   you do;
> And a little boy who's dreaming of the day
>   he'll be like you.
> You're the little fellow's idol. You're the wisest
>   of the wise;

In his little mind about you no suspicions ever
　　rise;
He believes in you devoutly, holds all you say
　　and do,
He will say and do, in your way, when he's
　　grown up just like you.
There's a wide-eyed little fellow who believes
　　you're always right;
And his ears are always open, and he watches
　　day and night.
You're setting an example, every day, in all you
　　do,
For the little boy who's waiting to grow up to
　　be like you.

Author Unknown

Your Child's Identity

Identity formation is more art than science. That is to say it is dynamic, relational, intuitive, subjective, and process-oriented. The shaping of a daughter's self-image is not as simple as programming a computer or changing the spark plugs in your car. The forging of your son's identity is far more complex than assembling his swing set or even filling out your tax return. Normally it takes years. It happens when you least expect it, like when you're cleaning her vomit out of the carpet, or when you're carrying your aging parent out of bed into the wheelchair, or while you're listening to your son rant and rave about his knuckleheaded science professor. Each of these everyday experiences communicates worth, dignity, and significance to your children as they watch you in action. Identity formation is the result of life-on-life parenting within the context of common ground. There are both tangible and intangible elements for identity formation. They are both essential in communicating worth to your child.

The Tangible Essentials

Time. There is no more vulnerable commodity in our lives than time. We judiciously use a Day Timer or Palm Pilot. Often from 6 A.M. to 6 P.M. we are booked! Time means money, opportunities, appointments. Managing time well means success. If we want to clearly communicate to our child her value to us, we will not only schedule priority time with her, we will also schedule extended time with her. There is no getting around it. I can honestly say there is nothing I enjoy more than the time I am able to spend with my children. This part of parenting for me is not a duty but a delight. While I think my children know I love them, it still remains my responsibility to continually remind them of it.

Talk. There is no substitute for verbally expressing to my child his value to me. It's not mushy or gushy or schmaltzy; it is essential. The words I use to describe my child become full-length mirrors in which he sees himself—for better or worse—so I diligently work at word selection so that the mirror I hold in front of him is accurate, encouraging, motivating, and empowering. More on this later.

Talent. The trap too many of us fall into is trying to impress our children with our strengths rather than expressing how impressed we are with their strengths. I know parents whose prowess at chess or Ping-Pong have unintentionally crushed their child's spirit. Sharing a talent with my daughter should be a time to encourage her, not dominate her. It doesn't take long in parenting when a child's personal talents will exceed Dad's and Mom's. Don't be threatened. Be delighted. I don't see Earl Woods disappointed that his son, Tiger, is a better golfer than he is.

Treasure. Raising a child costs a small fortune. If your life goal is saving money, you would do better by not having kids. Before our children graduate from college, many of us will face a million decisions and invest close to a million dollars. Bottom line is, what is worth more to me—a fat portfolio or a fulfilled child who loves me? What does it profit a person to gain a large investment portfolio and lose his own child?

When my kids were little, they killed all my young spring grass while playing on the swing hanging from the oak tree in the front yard. Initially I was angry, but then I caught myself and asked, *What is more important, raising healthy kids or raising healthy grass?* That's easy. When I am old and confined to a bed in a nursing home one day, my grass will not visit me. But my kids might.

Recently *Time* magazine carried a lead story on the brilliantly successful careers of top executive, late thirty-something, early forty-something women who are feeling terribly unfulfilled. Many of them never married or at least never had children. Now they have all the money in the world but no one to spend it on.

The Intangible Essentials

Accuracy. We want to make sure the mirrors built from the words we speak are true and accurate so that the reflection our child sees is real. In an effort to build their child's self-esteem, too many parents have sacrificed accuracy and have lost their child's confidence and trust. Your daughter can smell an insincere compliment a mile away. Your son knows when your accolades are hollow and patronizing. Insincere affirmation is like a curse. An honest appraisal, on the other hand, is a kiss on the lips.

Dignity. The moment your son or daughter was born, he or she possessed infinite worth and dignity. She did not need to qualify, perform, pass an entrance exam, or measure up. She was slapped on the back, took a deep breath, screamed loudly, and instantly was of immeasurable value. It was not a matter of doing; it was a matter of being. This means that a child's dignity, which was not gained by effort or performance, cannot be lost or sacrificed through behavior (or misbehavior). Every parent should remember that a primary parenting role is to continually affirm a child's innate worth and dignity. In a thousand ways we want to learn to say, "You are of infinite worth, and I want to demonstrate that to you by showing how much you mean to me, my son (my daughter)."

Integrity. Life without integrity or virtue is a barren wasteland. Virtue is what fills life with meaning, significance, purpose, and destiny. By *virtue* I mean the quality traits that civilizations have valued through the generations—morality, ethics, honesty, fidelity, creativity, sensitivity, humility, liberty, benevolence, kindness, love, selflessness, patriotism, family loyalty, perseverance, alertness, goodness, and service. When you draw a line at the bottom of this list and add them all up, the sum total is what we mean when we use the word *integrity.* It comes from the mathematical root word *integer,* meaning a whole number. Literally, *integrity* means being singleminded, centered, unduplicated. A person of integrity lives without hypocrisy, pretense, phony motives, or hidden agendas. The opposite is *duplicity*, which can be used to describe a person who has a double standard.

Identity. When we give our children accuracy—"This looks like you"—and dignity—"Your conduct is worthy"—and integrity—"Your actions are virtuous"—we are ready to say, "This is you!" This is what we mean by identity. Though identity goes beyond accuracy, dignity, and integrity, it is their logical extension. Without the other three, identity has a hollow ring; and the three without identity never quite hit home. The kiss never quite reaches the lips.

Identity is not based on what I do but rather on who I am. For that reason alone it has everything to do with acceptance—who I am, not who I want to be, wished I were, or never will be. Identity is take-it-or-leave-it who I am. It's based on the non-negotiables of life. And most tragically it is the non-negotiables that all too many children chafe against their whole lives. Just consider some of the obvious non-negotiables that clearly shape our identity:

mother	nation	genes	birth order
father	brothers	face	eyes
hand size	shoe size	grandparents	sisters
height	lips	sight	race
chin	ears	hair	culture
generation	voice	teeth	complexion
hearing	body build	metabolism	skin color
birth marks	special needs	handicaps	mental ability
scars	aging process	lifespan	religious background
extended family	status	parents' careers	nose
socioeconomic level	full name	meaning of one's name	

Every item on this list is more than a random, take-it-or-leave-it category. Each item significantly reflects an accurate view of my identity and similarly an accurate view of my child's identity. If these cannot be accepted, there is little hope for self-esteem elsewhere.

You Are My Son

The words "You are my Son" have identity written all over them. In one way or another, implicitly or explicitly, these four single-syllable words encompass at least half of the non-negotiables on our list—dad, mom, race, generation, nation, gender, birth order, brothers, sisters, grandparents, lifespan, neighborhood, full name, meaning of full name. In fact a case could be made for everything else on the list as well.

These are the words of Father God to Son God, four little words—well timed, well delivered, well intended, well received:

> *You*—Yes, you. I'm giving you my undivided attention, and I want your undivided attention. I'm talking to you, no one else. I have my eye on you, because I love to single you out. My hand is on you. My heart is set on you, you alone. This is uncompromised loyalty. I want you to realize that I never take my eye off you. Even when I'm not audibly talking to you, I'm watching, I'm caring, I'm protecting, I'm providing, just for you.

It was a tender voice, a kind, sensitive, loving voice, a strong, commanding, authoritative voice. The same voice that commanded the worlds into being, that spoke and the galaxies were made, is now singling out his one and only Son God.

> *Are*—You currently are; you always have been; you always will be. You are forever my Son. I know it is different for you being on earth. It is different for you not being with me here in heaven. But I just want to remind you that you are still as tight with me as you have ever been, since before time began, my Son.

My—I don't use this word lightly. You are mine. And I'm proud of it. I'm proud to call you mine and I'm proud to call myself yours. I love to be known as your Father. I don't have any other son like you—not a firstborn, not an uncreated, not from everlasting to everlasting, not any other Son God. There are not two or three others running around out there. You are mine; you are uniquely mine.

Son—You and I are uniquely and organically related, ontologically made out of the same God-stuff. Every ounce of deity in me is also in you. You are not just a chip off the old block; you are the Block, one and the same. You are the "spittin' image," very God of very God. Anyone who catches a glimpse of you has laid eyes on me. You have my DNA, my nature, my personality, my attributes, my character, my looks, my virtue, my dignity. Watching you brings me joy. Talking with you is the highlight of my day. *Son*—your identity is reflected in that word. Your security is found in being rightly related to me. I just want to remind you of who you are.

Can you taste it? Can you see the acceptance dripping from each word like dew from rose petals in the morning? Do you feel the kiss of the Father on the lips of the Son? Can you hear him chuckle with delight? Can you see Jesus' chest swell as he breathes in the aroma of his Dad's breath and savors the sanction of his Father's blessing? This is a rare moment—a holy moment. But hold the phone! This is a moment Father God desires for every single child that has ever been born. Think about it. Your son, your daughter need a kiss on the lips like this. They long to breathe in the full delight of your acceptance.

The Power of Unconditional Love

I happen to be a faith person. I have experienced firsthand the revolutionary, transformational power of God's unconditional love for me as tangibly demonstrated in the life of Jesus Christ. It radically impacts my life to know there is nothing that I can ever do that will make God love me any less. God forbid, if I were to commit adultery or take the life of another human being, my God would still love me just as much as he does right now. That fact blows my mind. And, perhaps even more amazing, there is nothing I will ever do to make God love me any more than he does right now. If I were to pray five hours a day or sell my house and give the entire wad of money to feed Ethiopian children, God could not possibly love me any more than he does this very second.

The effect this variety of unconditional love has on me— knowing there is nothing I can do to make God love me less and knowing there is nothing I can do to make him love me more—is to feel radically accepted for who I am. It makes me feel refreshingly invigorated to be all I can be and to respond passionately by showing this same radical unconditional love for those in my sphere of influence, particularly with those in my family for whom I care most.

Fred Is Not Fred

Accepting our children for who they are is radically different from making them who we want them to be. I will never forget the day I realized my son—my firstborn—was not me.

It was a Saturday, the second Saturday in March, which happened to be the first day of Little League tryouts. I was up early. My heart was beating fast. I could taste it—batting practice and fielding. I had rubbed oil into Fred's glove to soften it up, prepping for the new season. He'd had a great first year as a nine year old. Now that he was ten years old, he would dominate. The kid was great: coordinated, strong, big for his age. I could see his homeruns. I could feel the joy and pride of parenting fulfillment surging within. All this and his wake-up alarm hadn't even sounded yet.

I looked at my watch—8:00 A.M. *I'd better wake him up. Only an hour until tryouts,* I thought.

I strode into his room, flicked on the light, and announced with great confidence and anticipation, "Little League season starts today! It's time to get up, Fred!" He grunted something and rolled over.

With a full smile on my face, convinced that the message didn't get through, I spoke louder, "Fred, it's time to get up. I have a great breakfast ready for you—a Little League breakfast!"

I will never forget what happened next. I have replayed it in my mind a thousand times. It's like it all happened in slow motion. He sat up and leaned on one elbow. He squinted out of one bleary eye but was certainly in his right mind. He announced without apology, "I'm not going out for Little League this year." You could have blown me over!

What are you thinking? What are you saying? What are you doing? You must be joking, right? You're joking. You're kidding. You must be kidding. You're not kidding! These and fifty more thoughts like shots from an Uzi popped through my mind. Fortunately I didn't verbalize any of them. I stood there with my mouth open, speechless. He rolled over and pulled up his covers. His head flopped on the pillow, and he proceeded to sleep for a few more hours.

He slept right through the three hours of Little League tryouts. Make no mistake about it, those hours were three of the most painful and yet most important hours of my parenting life. It would have been easy for me to make the same mistake Lord Randolph Churchill made and put down my son for not giving baseball his all. It was during those three hours, however, that I came to grips with a number of essential parenting principles:

> While Fred has my name—he is Fred Allan Hartley IV and I am Fred Allan Hartley III—he is his own man.

> He is wired differently than I am. I would never have skipped a Little League season. In fact, if my parents had let me sleep through tryouts, I would have been furious.

> He makes his own choices according to his own temperament, personality, talents, and passions. It would be entirely inappropriate for me to make those choices for him. He does not exist to fulfill my ambitions, my goals, my purposes, or my passions. He exists to fulfill his own ambitions, goals, purposes, and passions.

> My role as dad is to help him discover what those purposes and passions are and to encourage him to pursue them.

> Bottom line, all this to say, parenting begins with my acceptance of who my child is, not who I want him to be, not who I think he is, not who I think he should become.

> Good parenting means I die to my ambition for him. He may have my gender, my looks, even my name, but that may be as far as the similarity goes. That doesn't mean for a moment that he will share my ambitions, my personality, or my values.

> Parenting begins with a big embrace for who my son is.

Acceptance says:

"I love you for who you are right now, not just for who you will become."

"I like you just the way you are, not for who I can make you be."

"I smile when I see you sleeping; even when you sleep through Little League tryouts."

"I embrace you for one simple, overarching reason—you are you and nobody else."

"You are one-of-a-kind, unique, special, significant."

"I would not trade you for anyone in this world."

"You are not perfect, but you are good enough for me."

"You are not perfect, but you are perfect for me."

"I take you as my son (daughter) not because of what you do but simply because you are my son (daughter)."

"I take you as my son (daughter) not because of what you accomplish—not because you get straight As, score a goal in the soccer game, win the science fair, or earn the scholarship to Yale University."

"I will love you if you pass or if you fail."

"I love you because you are you."

"There is nothing you will ever do to make me love you more."

"There is nothing you could ever do to make me love you less."

"You are you, and I'd lay down my life to defend your right to be the unique person you are."

"You are you, and I wouldn't take a billion dollars for you. In fact, if necessary, I'd give a billion dollars to protect your life and your individuality."

"You are without question one of the choicest gifts God has ever given to me."

"You are the best son (daughter) a dad (mom) could ever have."

"Just being with you—by your side—makes me feel rich. It gives me pleasure just to think about you."

"You are growing up well."

"I like the way God made you."

"You are unique."

"We share much in common, but you are your own person."

"You inspire me."

"I admire you."

"Watching you makes me feel like my life has been worth living."

"You give me hope."

"You are a winner!"

"I wouldn't trade you for anything in the world."

"I love watching you become your own person."

"I accept you for who you are."

"There is no one else who could ever take your place."

"Don't let others squeeze you into their mold."

"Be unique."

"Dare to be different."

"You can cut your hair however you want."

"You can listen to whatever music you want."

"You can make your own choices."

"I will still be your dad (mom) no matter what. If you end up behind bars—God forbid—I will never leave you; I will never forsake you."

"No matter how much you ever disappoint me—which you may never do—I will always be proud to be your dad (mom)."

I am a high D. *D* stands for decisive, dominant, determined, dedicated. I tell my wife it also stands for delightful. Sometimes she believes it, and sometimes she doesn't. Being a high D means that I tend to dominate relationships. I am a driver. When I take the DISC personality profile, my D is so high, the other letters don't even appear. If the test is a potential 20 points, I score a 21. In addition, I am a type A personality. That is, I am a high achiever.

When you combine my D and my A, it results in a potentially dangerous combination for parenting. Children don't like to be dominated. In fact let's go a step further. They don't need to be dominated. The truth is that children don't do well when dominated. The extent to which they are dominated is the extent to which they are not themselves. Domination is a kiss of death.

The opposite of domination is liberation. That would be a good first step for those who have been in the abusive pattern of domination. But there is a better way. Quite simply, it is called acceptance. Acceptance spawns creativity, individuality, independence, maturity, growth, dignity, and honor. All the virtues I as a parent long to see in my children thrive in the environment of acceptance.

Acceptance is my first responsibility to my daughter or son. And it is the primary longing within their bones. Deep down, embedded in their DNA, is the inner groaning for acceptance. *Don't mold me, slap me, or scold me. Don't break me, make me, or shape me. Just let me know that you accept me for who I am.*

If you listen carefully, you can hear your child pleading, *I may have been a girl when you wanted me to be a boy. I may look more like dad when you wanted me to look like mom. I may have been born when you were in your forties and hoping for no more kids. I may be more left-brained when you wanted me to be more right-brained. I may be strong-willed when you wanted me compliant. I may be more a "lion" personality, and you wanted me more an "otter." I may not be as athletically talented as you would have liked in a child, but please get over it. Just accept me for who I am. I know I'm not a finished product. I know I need your protection, your direction, and your correction. And, even when I don't show it, I really do deep down want it, but not until you demonstrate to me that you flat-out accept me for who I am.*

Before I will ever give you permission to help me revise the way I am motivated, I need to know for certain that you accept me for who I am, that you can handle it, that you rather like it, that you are glad I am the way I am. I may not say it audibly, and you may not hear it, but, believe me, I can tell intuitively whether or not you accept me.

Have you ever heard these words or something like them from your child?

Acceptance First

I can already feel some of you breathing heavily on my neck, raising objections like, "But what about when they mess up? I'm not supposed to accept that, am I?" Or, "Are you telling me that as a parent, I can't tell my children what's right and wrong? What about discipline and correction?" Good questions.

As parents, we not only have the right to advise, correct, discipline, rebuke, and train, we have the responsibility. In a later chapter we will see clearly how discipline communicates affection to a child when it is done appropriately. Right now it is essential that we establish a context of acceptance, which our child intellectually understands and intuitively trusts. Otherwise, efforts of discipline will be ineffective and potentially counterproductive.

You may ask, "Isn't there more to parenting than acceptance?" The answer is yes, there is more to parenting than acceptance. There is, however, no more to parenting than acceptance until you've communicated acceptance. In a sense, I am saying, "Not so fast. Don't rush it." Learn everything you can about acceptance, pure acceptance. Your child craves every ounce of acceptance he can get. He lives in a knockdown, stomp-in-the-ground, beat-'em-up, chew-'em-up, spit-'em-out world. That's his school, his neighborhood. That's his life, or so it seems from his end of the locker room.

Some days your daughter will return home from school beat up and abused. I don't necessarily mean physically abused, although that happens all too often. Sociologists tell us today that, tragically, one out of five girls will be date raped in college. Primarily, I am referring to emotional abuse. Verbally abused, her dignity, her self-esteem, her self-worth will crawl off the bus and up the driveway, bleeding, hemorrhaging. Some days she will need all the acceptance skills you can muster. Pitifully, in one fell swoop, a vicious word thrown like a dagger by a clumsy friend can drain all the lifeblood from the daughter you have spent years reinforcing.

Acceptance is no little thing. It is as life-essential as blood to the body or oxygen to the lungs. As parents you and I are the God-given rescue unit to be on call 24/7 to respond to his verbal or nonverbal emergency calls. When we learn to listen through the ear gate and the eye gate, we will be there to minister life when he feels as though he is losing it.

Self-Acceptance

One thing for sure—it's hard to give away what you don't have. Insecure people have a rough time making other people feel secure. Confused people have problems giving others peace of mind. Wounded people tend to wound others. They mock and abuse and drag others down. The blessed bless and the cursed curse.

You want your son and daughter to feel secure, to accept themselves, to be well adjusted. But what about you? What if you don't have a strong self-esteem? How are you supposed to infuse into your children what you yourself are struggling with?

We have all heard plenty of horror stories about generational curses, about alcoholic parents who raise angry kids in the angry domestic environment of their own frustrated lives. The curse goes on. Bummer. How do we break the cycle? Not an easy question. Simplistic answers are an insult to complex questions. We won't go there, but let me attempt to give a partial answer.

Am I a perfect parent? No, I'm not a perfect parent, not even close. And neither are you. Let me set the record straight right up front. Your child is not looking for perfect parents. In fact, perfect parents or even near-perfect parents would drive any imperfect kid up the wall. Kids are well aware of the fact that they are not perfect and even the notion that their parents might be perfect would be enough to drive them irreparably away from us.

Nope. No matter how you write the parenting job description, perfection isn't on it. No way. Instead, try words like human, mortal, reasonable, tender, compassionate, flexible, understanding, accepting, forgiving, humble, merciful, imperfect, growing, and maturing. Now those words ring true to any child.

Let's remember, freedom from perfection for parents is a two-way street. You are free from having to be perfect, and your children are free from having to be perfect as well. The good news is your kids are good enough for you. And you are good enough for them.

I have a theory. Parents who read parenting books tend toward perfectionism. They tend to be more the type A personality. Now, understand, I did not contract with George Barna to do a public survey of this theory. Although I'm confident that if I did, it would be verified. This means that we, more than most parents, need to take to heart the warning that perfectionism will drive our kids away.

The initial task of parenting, therefore, is not to mold, shape, conform, mentor, discipline, challenge, motivate, or lead. These are all important parts of parenting, but they are neither initial nor foundational. Parenting is actually far simpler than that. It is as simple as acceptance. Acceptance is the initial and foundational key to good parenting. It is as desirable to a child working on her postgraduate degree as it is to a pre-K child. Regardless of age, our children want to be sure one issue is locked in and secure. They want to know that they're accepted, and they want to know it over and over and over again.

Bedrock

We have almost finished talking about acceptance. You may feel as though you have a pretty good handle on it. You may feel ready to move on and tackle the next two areas—affection and affirmation. You may actually be chomping at the bit to move on. Not so fast! Let me warn you.

Affection will never be received by your daughter or son if she or he is unconvinced of your acceptance. And your affirmation will come across as clumsy, forced, and manipulative if there is not a bedrock of acceptance that undergirds the relationship. Acceptance gives us the relational currency to express affection in ways that say, "I embrace you for who you are, and I want you to know how deeply I feel about you." And then it enables us to speak powerfully and affirmatively, "I am so proud of you," in a way that will ring true.

If my child hears my affirmation without hearing my acceptance, he will always feel as though he needs to perform to gain my favor. And performance is a treadmill made for rats or gerbils, not children. If my child hears my affection without my acceptance, she will think I love her for me and not for her, and to this she will react. No child wants to feel as though he exists simply to meet some emotional need in his parents' life. "Love me as me," our child says, "not for how I make you feel."

These words and sentiments are not cruel. They are honest. They are even appropriate. Our children do not exist primarily to make us feel good about ourselves. Nor do they exist to fulfill our dreams or ambitions. For this reason, acceptance must be firmly established first. It is the common ground from which all parenting is done. Our sons and daughters must feel our acceptance, our embrace, just for who they are, before they feel our affection or our affirmation. They need to be convinced of it emotionally and intellectually, objectively and subjectively. Acceptance becomes the emotional currency of any and every relationship. And it must not be assumed in the home; it is actually more important to express it in the home.

As Dad or Mom, you have a unique role in your child's life to help with his or her identity formation. You will face your own opening-day-of-Little-League moments when you will need to wrestle with how you will respond to your child's uniqueness in contrast to your own. Remember, perfection is one requirement you can remove from your parenting résumé. Aren't you glad?

Here are some questions that will help you measure the level of your acceptance of your child:

Can I legitimately say that I accept my daughter for who she is?

Do I tell her?

Do I regularly communicate to my son his unique identity?

Have I ever felt as distant from him as Lord Randolph did from his son, Winston?

Have I ever spoken hurtful, angry words that left my child wounded? If so, have I mended the fences?

Have I identified common ground with my child? Am I building a relationship on it?

In the next chapter we will discover one of the greatest powers we have as parents. Learning to use it effectively will enable you to fill your child's acceptance tanks and watch him or her become the young man or young woman God intends.

A Window into My Child's Heart:
Feeling Honored

One of the ways my dad shows his love for me is through a couple of nicknames he's given me—pet names he has for me and no one else.

Throughout my childhood he called me "Cruiser." My body is built to endure long distances in running. I have always been very fast. I remember countless times running five miles around Stone Mountain with my dad. The nickname has given me great confidence in my athletic abilities.

Now that I have entered my teenage years, Dad has given me another nickname—he calls me his "Prince." "Cruiser" was a great nickname, but "Prince" has taken this name thing to a different level. When he tells me that I am his Prince, there is an indescribable feeling that goes on inside of me. It means so much when my dad comes into my room at night, flops down on my bed, and calls me his Prince. The name reminds me of honor, royalty, next in line, and being special, and it makes me want to be all that God wants me to be.

My dad really knows how to make me feel good about myself.

Stephen Hartley, age sixteen

3

I Honor You

I can live for two months on a good compliment.

Mark Twain

Whether we realize it or not, the value we attach to God, our children, and ourselves greatly determines the success or failure of all our relationships. Indeed, nothing will do more to shape lives than to give and receive.

Gary Smalley and John Trent

The greatest power a parent has is the power of blessing. I deliberately did not say *one* of the greatest powers a parent has, because I sincerely believe there is no greater power given to parents than the power, privilege, and authority to influence their own child through well-chosen, accurate words of affirmation. I am also convinced that it is the most underutilized parenting tool.

When I was in graduate school, both my friend and I became fathers for the first time. We both had sons, giving us an additional bond. He had a neat habit of putting his hand on his baby boy's head every night, looking him square in the eyes, and speaking a blessing. As he was explaining this to me, I asked him, "What do you mean, a blessing?"

He gave me a few examples. "Every night I go in his room and say something like, 'William, your name means "leader, helmet." You will become a great leader of men. Good night, my son.' Or, 'You are my pride and joy. Your daddy and mama love you. You are the best gift God could have ever given us. Sleep well, my son.'"

Every night he followed the same, healthy pattern. He varied the words but consistently spoke a strongly favorable blessing to his boy.

Some time before graduating, due to a heavy schedule of late-night cramming for exams, the pattern was broken. One night he went in his son's room, pulled up the covers, and was turning to leave when something happened he would never forget. He felt his son's hand clasp his forefinger. What happened next gives me goose bumps to write. Little William tugged his dad's hand up to his little forehead. His little eyes looked up longingly as if to say, *Please, bless me, Daddy. I love it when you bless me. You won't leave my room tonight without blessing me, will you, Daddy?*

This is a powerful picture of every child's heart. This is an X ray of what permeates your son's or daughter's soul. The longing to be blessed is ingrained in every chromosome in your child's body, with every beat of his heart.

Let me interject a thought at this point regarding peer pressure. Too often we approach peer pressure from a negative perspective. It is true there is negative peer pressure, but there is also positive peer pressure. Every child tends to run toward those who cheer the loudest. If their friends outcheer their parents, it should come as no surprise when internally they begin to run away from home.

A Real Blessing

Kerry Collins wears number five for the New York Giants. He strutted into Super Bowl XXXV in Tampa Bay with quite a remarkable season under his belt. Ever since they discovered he had a gun for an arm in high school, he had been quarterbacking football teams and winning big. But this particular day in Tampa Bay was one of the worst quarterback performances in Super Bowl history. He threw the ball 39 times, completing a mere 15 passes for a meager 112 yards, 4 interceptions, and zero touchdowns. After that you would expect Kerry to be down on himself, and yet he said it was one of the happiest days of his life. Why? Because that evening was virtually the first time in his adult life when all four members of his nuclear family were in the same room together, even if it did happen to be the Tampa Bay stadium. After the big game he stood in the tunnel with his dad, Pat, his mom, Roseanne, and his older brother, Patrick. "It was kind of amazing to see all of us in the same room again, but we were so happy to see Kerry so happy," his brother said.[1]

When his folks got a divorce during Kerry's adolescence, it was painful for everyone involved. The pressure to win became more dominant for the young quarterback than the joy of winning, so he started drinking. *Sports Illustrated* noted, "The drinking led to hating himself and the hating himself led to hurting himself." This particular day was the culmination of a tumultuous life and a budding career. He had overcome the

DUI, the racist allegation, the nicknames like "Vodka Collins." He had dealt with his bitterness toward his dad and with his estrangement from his mom. Kerry added, "We are not the Brady Bunch, but we're doing okay. I'm back to being a son to my mom again. And that means a lot to me."[2]

Did you hear that—"a son to my mom again"?

His mother said, "I just sat him next to me and said, 'Don't go anywhere. Let me just stare at you.'"

Kerry added, "I found out winning doesn't make you a good person, and losing doesn't make you a bad person. Nothing can happen to me on a football field now that can affect me. My worst day sober is better than my best day drunk."[3]

These are words of a blessed soul, words from a man whose parents weren't perfect—just perfect for him. It was as if, when he took off his helmet after the game and walked down the tunnel toward the locker room, his dad and mom greeted him, held him, and placed on his forehead their hands of blessing. A son again—that is better than a Super Bowl ring any day.

Gary Smalley and John Trent wrote an insightful parenting book called *The Blessing* in which they isolate five essential elements to a blessing. Their description of these elements is worth a brief review.[4]

Touch

Doctors tell us the body contains five million touch receptors, one third of which are located in the palms of our hands. These receptors are nerve endings that receive and relay the sense of touch. Dr. Krieger of New York University has published medical reports showing that the body's hemoglobin blood count increases through the laying on of hands. If there is evidence that physical touch is beneficial physiologically, it is certainly easy to imagine that touch would be beneficial personally and psychologically as well.

A reporter for the *New York Times* interviewed Marilyn Monroe about her being shuffled from foster home to foster home throughout her childhood. "Did you ever feel loved by any of the foster homes with whom you lived?" he asked. This enchanting woman, loved by millions, pitifully announced, "Once, when I was about seven or eight. The woman I was living with was putting on makeup. She was in a happy mood. So she reached over and patted my cheek with the rough puff. For that moment, I felt loved by her." The reporter noted that Miss Monroe had tears in her eyes as she remembered that moment.[5]

Can you imagine? The woman who symbolized love to a generation was herself so starved for love as a child that her fondest memory was a glancing touch of a powder puff from a lone foster mom.

How do you touch your son or daughter appropriately and lovingly?

Audible Communication

When we say nothing to our child, he or she is left to fill in the blanks. If we want to convey blessings to our child, we'd better verbalize them. Even though it is possible to bless our child in a variety of ways without words, regardless of how else the blessing is communicated, it is always a little better when it is audibly reinforced. "Thanks for picking me up after practice, Mom." "I'm glad to do it," she replies, "because I love you."

On screen, Sylvester Stallone projects an impervious, tough-guy veneer. Hear the hurt in his masculine soul from his childhood.

My parents had their difficulties so there wasn't any time for me or my younger brother. It wasn't a tranquil household. There was great chaos. My father was an extraordinarily exacting man, and if what you did wasn't a photocopy of the way he did it, then you had no abilities and had to be chastised and corrected. And quite often the correction was, you know, shocking. He made me feel extraordinarily inept. "Why can't you be smarter?" "Why can't you be stronger?" I didn't have one virtue. He never said he was proud of me.[6]

As fans of golf, my son and I sat glued to the 1999 U.S. Open at Pinehurst No. 2 as Payne Stewart drained his final putt on the eighteenth green to win the title. A year later we could hardly believe our eyes as we watched a private plane flying off course, apparently having lost cabin pressure, knowing that Payne and a couple of his buddies were in that plane. As feared, they had all died. When his wife, Tracey, published his biography, the dedication read, "To Chelsea and Aaron, may this book be a permanent reminder of your wonderful father and how much he loved you both. May you both live with a similar sense of love, joy, adventure and enthusiasm for life. I love you, Mum."[7] Tracey Stewart wisely preserved her husband's passion for life and love for his children so that, even in his death, he could speak to both of them.

Attribute High Value

Carefully chosen words have the ability to heal broken hearts, lift downcast spirits, and mend shattered egos, particularly when spoken by mothers or fathers whose hearts are wired to their son or daughter. Never underestimate the power of a single, sincere expression of worth spoken to one we love.

Picture a Special Future

High school coaches, teachers, youth pastors, and parents all share the same opportunity—to plant a vision of hope in the heart and mind of an impressionable young person. Vision and hope are like Miracle-Gro for the human spirit; pour them on a wilted spirit, stand back, and watch it perk up right before your eyes!

Active Commitment to Fulfill the Blessing

Teammates can give needed motivation to their quarterback when they assure him, "We're here for you. Take charge and lead us to victory." Soldiers who tell their commanding officer, "Sir, we will stand with you, loyally serving under your command," encourage their leader in the face of battle. And our child needs to hear our wholehearted support as she faces seemingly insurmountable odds each day.

Trent and Smalley reference the traditional Jewish habit of regular, even weekly, family blessings. The father will light a candle for each family member. The children will come around the mother, lay hands on her, and speak a blessing. Parents in turn will place their hands on each child and speak a personal, distinct blessing on each child.[8]

I can hear some readers already objecting, "Okay, enough with the lighting of candles and the touchy-feely stuff. That's not for me." As my kids say to me, "Relax!" I don't light candles either, but I am sold on giving the blessing.

What Is a Blessing?

A blessing is affirmation with an attitude—a positive attitude. It's affirmation with the afterburners on, affirmation with an adrenaline rush.

A blessing is everything I ever wanted yet never dreamed possible. It's finding out I am who I intuitively thought I was, yet never knew anyone else agreed with me. It's permission to become the person I was meant to be. Blessing is wind in my sails, wings beneath my feet, fire in my engine. Blessing is power, sheer power.

Bestowing blessing is the greatest power we as parents possess, and we want to learn to use it effectively on behalf of our children. Blessing is what a mother bird does to her young when she nudges them out of the nest and says, "Go ahead. You can fly." It's the loving hand on the head and the affirming words that follow—words, as I said in the last chapter, that are characterized by four essential elements: accuracy, dignity, integrity, and identity.

You and I want our child to feel special because he or she *is* special. He is a one-of-a-kind, handcrafted, designer edition, an original. A primary role we have as parents is to accurately shape our child's identity. We would do her a disservice to either downplay or exaggerate her personhood.

I want my children to receive the blessing, to grow up knowing who they are and who they were meant to be. I want nothing more than that they celebrate their unique personhood and realize the full extent of their God-given potential. For all these reasons, I want to use what limited resources I have to influence my child to enter in and wholeheartedly celebrate his or her uniqueness.

If our children adopt a shrunken view of themselves, it will cause an inferiority problem. Adopting an inflated view of themselves will cause a superiority problem. In the middle is the accurate, sober, realistic, healthy viewpoint, which we want our children to celebrate and enjoy.

Soon after we celebrated Fred's one-year birthday in grand fashion, Sherry chuckled quietly so as not to interrupt the moment. She pointed at Fred, "Check him out!" He was engrossed with his own reflection in a full-length wall mirror. He was chuckling, cackling, completely oblivious to everything else going on around him. Enthralled with the reflection of his own face in the mirror, he licked the mirror, kissed the mirror, drooled and slobbered on the mirror. He hopped, skipped, and danced, but he never took his eyes off himself. He unashamedly, unselfconsciously, unrelentingly loved what he saw. Sherry and I were captured by his performance. I quietly whispered to her, "Let's hope he always loves himself this much for the rest of his life."

That is every parent's dream—for their children to love, accept, and understand themselves. This certainly has nothing to do with self-infatuation, arrogance, or twisted vanity. This is a healthy self-image and self-acceptance we all want our children to possess.

Words of Blessing

If the ear gets the trophy as the most important parenting tool in the body, the tongue finishes a close second. Once the ear has done its initial work of fact-finding, asking the right questions, and gathering relevant information, the tongue is adequately prepared to swing into action. The tongue is out of danger of shooting from the hip or shooting in the dark when it has been tamed and tutored by the ear. The Bible says, "The tongue has the power of life and death" (Prov. 18:21). That is certainly true; however, if we listen well, our tongue is more likely to bring life.

When do we start saying words of blessing? Infancy works. We can even bless our child prenatally. Countless parents want to get their child on the fast track of blessing. They place their hands on the mother's extended tummy and speak blessing to the preborn baby in the womb. It's never too soon to begin speaking words of acceptance, affection, and affirmation.

Many parents of junior high students often panic because they suddenly realize they have not utilized the power of blessing and they see that regrettable negative patterns have already become somewhat entrenched in their children. If that's the case for you, cut your losses and start now. It may sound awkward to your child; it may feel awkward to you. But like a good golf swing, it will feel and look better with practice.

Words of blessing can be words of acceptance, affection, or affirmation. Here are some examples of blessings we can say to our children in each of these categories. When reading, it is easy to scan or even skip lists and jump to the next section. I appeal to you to courageously resist that temptation now. I ask you to read carefully the following three lists of blessings. These have been diligently collected and utilized over the years. Very few are original with me, but when I used them, I assure you, they came from my heart.

Blessings of Acceptance

"You know what I like about you?" (*Pause.*) "Everything!"

"I'm so glad you are my daughter (my son)."

"I love to spend time with you."

"You're my hero, champion, favorite golf partner, my prince, my princess" (use your own pet name).

"Watching you makes me feel like my life has been worth living."

"I want you to tell me how you think I am doing as your mom (or dad). I will just listen. No interruptions. I want you to tell me what you think I do well and where I need to improve."

"You're the best!"

"I know you will grow up, but for now, I like you just the way you are."

"I admire you for _____."

"You know, when I was listening to your conversation with your friends, I was taking notes. You were taking me to school. You really took a stand. That was an example to me. Way to go!"

Blessings of Affection

(To Sons)

"You are a handsome dude!"

"You da man!"

"I love you!"

"You are a good guy."

(To Daughters)

"I haven't told you lately, but you are beautiful. You really are."

"I'm not sure if you like hearing me say it, but you are really beautiful."

"I love you."

"You will make some lucky guy an incredible wife some-day."

"I don't know how we'll ever find a guy good enough for you."

(Sons or Daughters)

"I love being with you."

"I miss you."

"You have a great heart."

"You are a great person."

"Your heart is as good as gold."

"I feel with you. I know how you feel."

"I feel a little of what you're feeling; tell me more."

"I'm not sure I can feel all that you're feeling, but tell me more."

"I respect how you feel. I know this is so very difficult."

"I don't blame you at all for feeling that way. I'm sure I would too if I were you."

Blessings of Affirmation

"I'd rather watch you play soccer than just about anything else in the world."

"The best thing I do all week is to get to watch you play basketball on weekends."

"You are smart. When I was your age, I wasn't reading books like that."

"I am proud of those grades you've gotten."

"I hated to miss the awards banquet. I want to watch the video." (You can't get away with this one too often.)

"Hey, I switched my schedule so I could be at your awards banquet."

"You are caring (kind, patient, self-disciplined, sensitive, honest, creative)."

"Way to go!"

"You have tremendous leadership skills."

"I heard the nicest thing about you today." (Tell him or her about it.)

"I don't necessarily agree with your decision, but I admire the process you went through to consider various options."

"You are amazing! I could never have done that when I was your age."

"You would have run rings around me when I was your age."

If you are not accustomed to communicating verbal blessings such as these, I recommend not pouring them on too fast, especially at first. Go easy. Let it flow naturally. Compliments need to come from within. They need to flow from your mind and your heart. If you feel clumsy or awkward, the words will sound hollow or contrived. In fact, if you have neglected the power of blessing, even if you now see its value and feel natural in speaking, things may initially still sound hollow or contrived to your child. The human spirit at times feels awkward initially when affirmed, particularly when it has been blessing-deprived. Dr. James Dobson gives us all a reality check:

> The average amount of time spent by . . . middle-class fathers with their small children was thirty-seven seconds per day! Their direct interaction was limited to 2.7 encounters a day, lasting ten to fifteen seconds each! That represented the contribution of fatherhood for millions of America's children in the 1970s, and I believe the findings would be even more depressing today.[9]

If this sounds like you, then you'll need to work on spending more time with your child as you begin to speak blessings to him.

The Blessing of Identity

Identity is more than a concept; it's rocket fuel. Identity is power—sheer power. It is stronger than a locomotive. It is faster than a speeding bullet. It is able to leap tall buildings in a single bound. It's the power to stay the course when weaker souls drop along the roadside, wander off looking for a fast-food restaurant, or cry for mama. It's the power to keep our oath even when it hurts. It's the resolve, the determination to fight the good fight, to finish the race, to win the prize. Identity is the face set like flint. Identity is what every parent wants for his or her girl or boy, yet too few parents carefully craft their child's identity.

I want to run two videos for you to more adequately illustrate this concept of identity. One video was made in Hollywood; the other took place upstairs in my son's bedroom.

Video number one, *Gladiator*, is certainly no chick flick. It's high on testosterone and high on identity. Every character is oversized. Maximus, the effective commander of the Roman army, is much loved by his men. He exemplifies the motto shared by his troops, "Strength and honor." He is pitted against Commodus, who usurps the throne by strangling his aging father, emperor Marcus Aurelius, ravaging Maximus's wife and only son, and ordering Maximus killed. Commodus is a picture of weakness and dishonor.

In one of the all-time world-class self-identifying moments, Maximus is asked his name. Emperor Commodus is certain Maximus has been long dead. In front of a standing-room-only, cheering Colosseum, the weak-hearted emperor walks down from his prominent throne, down onto the blood-stained dirt floor, where the gladiators have demonstrated incredible valor, and demands that the victorious gladiator identify himself. The tension builds as the unknown self-effacing hero attempts to remain anonymous. After the emperor's insistence, the hero states, "My name is Gladiator," and he commits a social crime—he turns to walk away.

"How dare you turn your back to me! Slave! You will remove your helmet and tell me your name!" the flustered Commodus demands.

Slowly, intentionally, dramatically, Maximus lifts his helmet and reveals his face to a shocked, speechless emperor. The words spill from deep within the hero's soul. He speaks words of self-identity, words of strength and honor, words of confidence that make you shiver as they are spoken. Listen carefully to the precision of his self-disclosure. "My name is Maximus Decimus Meridius, commander of the armies of the North, general of the Felix Legions, loyal servant to the true emperor Marcus Aurelius, father of a murdered son, husband to a murdered wife, and I will have my vengeance in this life or in the next."

I love that. It came like a tidal wave crashing over Commodus and the entire Colosseum. It swept over lesser souls and carried them in its wake. But where does an answer like that come from? It comes from deep within a man, from years of accumulated virtue, from many healthy relationships, particularly from a dad or a mom who spoke blessing into the tender, impressionable soul of his or her son during the formative years.

Video number two took place in our home one night around 10 P.M., long after my nine-year-old son should have been asleep. I arrived home after a long day. Following a little smooch with my wife, I asked, "The boys still awake?" "Go up and see," she answered.

After bounding up the stairs two or three at a time, I whispered, "Psst! Andrew, you awake?" Silence. Next bedroom, "Stephen, you awake?"

"Yeah, Dad, come on in."

After the usual how-was-your-day routine, I said, "Tell me something about your day that made it special." Stephen is our talker. Of all our children, he is the one my parents most enjoy talking with on the phone, because they get the most Hartley trivia from him.

"Well, Dad, we had an awesome chapel today. The speaker talked on Stephen in the Bible." He got serious, reflective. His little chin started quivering. Somewhere deep inside, Stephen's integrity must be connected to his chin, because whenever he's about to say something deeply significant, his chin always gives you a clue that it is coming. "Stephen was the first one killed in the early church. He was a martyr, Dad." His little chin started twitching more than usual. He swallowed hard. His eyes moistened. Then he said something I will never forget no matter how long I live. "And, Dad, someday," he swallowed hard again, "someday, Dad, I would be willing to die for Jesus too."

As I looked at my third child, second son, I thought, *This is from God. This is a holy moment. He is expressing a deep sense of identity, a deep conviction in his soul.* I looked at him with great admiration and a sense of wonder. This was more than a rote Sunday school answer. This was more than something he learned from a kid's flannel-graph Bible story. This was huge. He was so deeply, intimately, wholeheartedly identifying with the worth of Jesus Christ, God's only Son, that he would be willing, if asked, to put his own life on the line. This had nothing to do with his dad being a pastor. It had nothing to do with trying to please his parents. God had worked so deeply in his little heart that our son had chosen to please Christ over preserving his own life.

All I could do was swallow hard and affirm his conviction. "Stephen, if you ever have the chance, don't miss it! There is nothing that would ever make your mom and dad more proud of you." We hugged, then I blessed him.

I slowly, deliberately, almost reverently walked downstairs. It was one of those rare parenting moments when I felt like I was on holy ground. When I told Sherry this story, she cleared her throat and reminded me, "You know, we named him after the Stephen in the Bible. And his name means 'Crown.' He is quite a little prince."

From that moment on, my pet name for Stephen has been "Prince." Frequently I go into his room, flop down on the bed next to him, and ask, "How's the Prince?" He is a prince. Knowing this about himself is strength and honor for Stephen. It is identity.

Identity surfaces through some of the wonderful, serendipitous moments of family life. You can't put it in a jar. You can't buy it on Ebay. You can't predict when it will surface. But when it does, it is more precious than just about anything in the world. For everything else there is MasterCard.

In helping your child discover, embrace, and celebrate his unique identity, it may be helpful to photocopy and complete with your child the following inventory. It's not an SAT that will evaluate his competency or place him in a percentile. The only wrong answers are inaccurate answers. Be encouraged in the process and, equally important, be encouraging.

Just as a person's DNA is already developed in childhood, so is her personality. It is encouraging—even invigorating— to trace a child's formation, personality, passions, interests, unique gifting, and identity from infancy, through childhood, and on into adulthood. As the Bible notes, "Even a child is known by his actions" (Prov. 20:11).

Most important, we want to help our child discover who he really is and embrace and celebrate his own uniqueness. Your child may be so far from drooling over himself in the mirror that this exercise may be painful—even frustrating.

Again, take your time, remembering that your child is asking big questions:

"Am I okay?"

"Am I normal?"

"Am I handsome (pretty)?"

"Am I funny?"

"Am I smart?"

"Am I coordinated?"

"Am I likeable?"

First name (and name meaning):

Middle name (and name meaning):

Last name (and name meaning):

Gender:

Birth order:

Interests:

Gifted in these areas:

    Intellectual

    Academic—specifically: _____

    Athletic—specifically: _____

    Creative arts—specifically: _____

    Musical

    Relational/social skills

    Spiritual interest

    Leadership

    Organizational

Early accomplishments:

Elementary teachers' affirmation:

Coaches' comments:

Personality type (either DISC or Myers-Briggs[10]):

Personal interests/ passions:

"Am I socially acceptable?"

"Am I loveable?"

"Am I lovely?"

Developing an accurate self-image may take your child a while. It may be more like completing a fine oil painting than taking a photograph. Be patient. It's a process. And while her image is gradually taking form, you'll want to be in her corner cheering. Your child is waiting for you to place your hand of blessing on her head. If you miss your opportunities, you may be left with a pain that never goes away.

Billy and Ruth Graham watched patiently as their son Franklin's image was developing. In Franklin's biography, *Rebel with a Cause*, we get an idea of how patient they had to be. He does not paint his family as perfect, but his account reveals a family with honor, integrity, security, and authenticity. During his childhood, Franklin spent a lot of time with his dad, shooting a 22-caliber rifle into walnut trees, taking long hikes, and traveling with him. But he also tells about his rebellion against his parents' way of life. He jokes, "If my mom has white hair, it's because of me!"

Ruth and Billy wrote the afterword to their son's book. Notice the virtues expressed in their words: "Watching Franklin grow up has been an experience. Nothing like being fascinated with your own son's life. A lot of what is contained in this book we had never heard before. However, under all this rebel reminiscing, this book fails to tell you of the tender side of the little boy growing up." They go on to tell about joyful and fun times, and they candidly admit that there were difficult times, the rebellious years, the smoking behind closed doors. They end by saying, "With God, nobody's hopeless."[11] Those are encouraging words for all of us.

Here are some questions to ponder:

Have you discovered the power of blessing your son or daughter?

Have you learned to verbally hug your child?

Do you frequently see the look in your child's face that says, *Wow! That felt great. Thanks for honoring me for who I am!*

PART 2

Meeting Their Need for Affection

I Love You

Affection. Not gushy-mushy sentimentalism, not Hollywood sensationalism, just down-to-earth, honest-to-goodness, unconditional positive regard expressed in terms that ring true is what a child needs.

Let's face it. The three words "I love you" can sound trite and threadbare. Worse than that, your child may currently be in an "Awww-come on! I-hate-it-when-you-tell-me-you-love-me" frame of mind. Or he may have a "Yuck! Don't-ever-hug-me-again-in-public" attitude. Don't panic. Most youth go through that phase and often what they are trying to say is, "You are not speaking my love language."

When Father God told his Son, "I love you," it struck a deep chord in his soul. Had he forgotten his Daddy's love? Probably not. Was this the first time he'd heard the words from his Daddy's lips? No way. But no matter how many times a child hears the words "I love you," they are music to dance to. Like sitting down to our favorite meal, it tastes good every time. There is no doubt about it; the Father's love is what the Son lived for.

Your child's soul was made to feed on affection—*your* affection in particular. These three words, when appropriately communicated in terms she understands, will meet a need way down deep in the recesses of her inner life. More than any other single factor, your love for your child sets the tempo for her intimacy potential. These next four chapters will help you express "I love you" in ways your child will understand.

A Window into My Child's Heart:
Belonging

Some of my favorite family memories come not only from our family vacations but from the hours logged traveling to and from our vacation spot. It was on one such trip that we were traveling all the way up the east coast from Miami, Florida, to Maine. (Let me remind you, that is a very long way for six people in a minivan!)

Before we got on the interstate, McDonald's Egg McMuffins still on our laps, Dad announced from the driver's seat that he had a very important "vacation declaration" to make. Our ears perked up expectantly, awaiting some exciting information. Dad continued, "There is a new rule I hereby establish on this vacation. If any of us—Mother and myself included—is caught taking himself or herself too seriously, being too uptight, tense, stressed, edgy, anxious, or rigid on this vacation, we all have the right to say to each other, 'Chill out! Don't take yourself so seriously!'" He explained that if someone says this to us, we should not take offense but rather appreciate the gentle nudge and reconsider our attitude.

I can remember looking around the van—everyone was smiling at each other. We all liked the idea.

Needless to say, the phrases "Chill out!" and "Don't take yourself so seriously!" were used quite a bit on that vacation; in fact they have become buzz words during each of our family vacations since. They are loving words of advice we freely offer one another. They give us children equal ground with our parents on which we can appeal without being disrespectful. Usually they bring a smile and a "Thanks, I needed that."

Andrea

4

I Like You

Never underestimate a gesture of affection.

Max Lucado

If you live to be a hundred, I want to live to be a hundred minus one day, so I never have to live without you.

Winnie the Pooh

Barney is a good friend and one of the most affectionate men I know. Not overbearing or intense, he is just legitimately warm, infectious, personable. More important, he is a great dad, world class. I invited him to talk to a group of young parents. He gave us one parenting tip that day I will never forget. When he said it, every parent's head in the room nodded and most mouths dropped open. You could almost hear a bell ring—ca-ching!

"When I'm alone with one of my children and I want him to feel my unconditional affection for him," he said, "I look him square in the eye. You have to be sure he is looking back at you for this to have its full effect. Then when we have locked eye-balls, I pop the question, 'Do you know what I like about you?' By now the child knows what is coming. He gives me this huge smile from ear to ear. He knows the answer but he never says it. He just sits there as if waiting for a good backrub. I say it the same way every time. No matter how often I do it, he enjoys it just as much. After I ask him the question, 'Do you know what I like about you?' we stare at each other for an enriching second, and then I simply say, 'Everything!'" Ca-ching!

Don't you like that? I love it. It rings true. In one way or another, we want to communicate to our children a healthy, wholehearted embrace of their person. "Do you know what I like about you? Everything!" is like a kiss, a hug. It oozes acceptance and affection. It brims over with blessing. It puts our arms around them and says, "You're not perfect, but you're good enough for me!"

I-Like-You Parenting

There is a definite distinction between I-*love*-you parenting and I-*like*-you parenting. I-love-you parenting is more all-inclusive, more bottom-line, more all-encompassing, more essential to fulfilling the God-given role we play in our child's life. This is the more traditional style of parenting, which says, "You're my child. I gave life to you. My primary role is to protect you and provide for you."

I-like-you parenting, however, is more fun, more spontane-ous, more enjoyable. This side of parenting says, "I want to be your friend, your buddy, your pal. I don't want to play the heavy all the time. I want a give-and-take relationship of equality."

It may help to see these two approaches side by side:

I-Love-You Parenting	I-Like-You Parenting
You are my child.	You are my friend.
You bring me fulfillment.	You bring me enjoyment.
I am related to you.	I can relate to you.
You are family.	You are fun.
I am your protector, provider, parent.	I am your cheerleader, buddy, pal.
You receive from me.	I receive from you.
We have distinct roles.	We have equal roles.
I gave you life.	You give me joy.
More all-encompassing.	More superficial.

Make no mistake about it, "I love you" beats "I like you." As we will see in the next two chapters, I love you is the I'll-go-the-distance, the I'll-do-what-it-takes commitment that separates parental love from the rest of the field and puts it in a league all by itself. As we can see in the table, however, the I-love-you and the I-like-you aspects of our relationship both have merit. We don't need to argue one against the other and settle for an either-or. We want a both-and.

In their twenty-nine-month bestseller *Built to Last: Successful Habits of Visionary Companies*, James Collins and Jerry Porras studied thirty-six hundred years of corporate experience and discovered four universal principles that separate the gold-medal companies from the bronze.[1] Their six-year study considered two hundred of the top Fortune 500 companies. They identified one of the four principles as "the genius of the and, not the tyranny of the or." If ever we want to take hold of the power of the and, it is on behalf of the family. If ever we want something built to last, it is the family.

Paradoxically, I hear people trying to argue liking and loving against each other: "I love them, but I don't like them." Or they even try to get religious about it: "I have to love them, but I don't have to like them." That sounds pious, but I don't know what it means. It sounds like double talk. What message are we sending our children when we say, "I can't wait until summer vacation is over and the kids go back to school" or "I wish you'd get a job and get out of the house"? Most people can intuitively feel whether we like them, and if they come to the conclusion that we don't, they are certainly suspicious of any expression of our love, especially if they are our children.

It should be easy to determine that both sides of parenting are important even though there is an obvious left-to-right progression. I-love-you parenting precedes and supercedes I-like-you parenting. A proper understanding of these two important aspects of parenting can potentially save oodles of counseling bills during the teen years. So many parents put themselves over an artificial barrel trying to be their child's friend. Why? Because they are choosing I-like-you to the exclusion of I-love-you parenting, trying to be a pal instead of a parent. Consequently, they forfeit much of their child's security in the process. This concept will come into even clearer focus in the next chapter.

When we appropriately merge *liking* our child with *loving* our child, it creates a winning atmosphere in which children thrive. In this chapter, I will suggest many practical ways of infusing your home with healthy doses of laughter, value, and mutual respect, which make up healthy family life. You show me a healthy family, and I will show you a family that enjoys being together.

Imagine assembling the members of your nuclear family for an "open forum." There is one item of business on the agenda to discuss: "Do we want to be an I-like-you family or an I-don't-like-you family?" Obviously we would anticipate a unanimous vote for an I-like-you family. However, all too many homes are functioning in the negative. They are I-don't-like-you families. Take inventory of your own home life according to the following chart.

An I-Like-You Family	An I-Don't-Like-You Family
We schedule time with each other.	We don't schedule time together.
We have fun together.	We don't have fun together.
We play games.	No games.
We do hobbies and recreation together.	No group recreation.
We enjoy family traditions, particularly at holidays.	We have few traditions.
We enjoy vacations together.	Family vacations are a drag.
We look for excuses to celebrate.	We seem unable to celebrate.
Our home is full of healthy laughter.	Our home is full of anger.
We laugh at ourselves.	We mock each other.
We intentionally off-load stress.	Our home is a pressure cooker.
We enjoy each other.	We tolerate each other.
We look forward to getting home.	We look forward to getting away.
We have long conversations.	We only rarely have meaningful conversations.

I-like-you families are healthy families. Mutual respect, joy, and security characterize these homes. They are established on five building blocks.

Building Block 1: Celebration

If you want to have fun and enjoy each other, it is helpful to have a catalyst, a rally point, a reason to celebrate. Some families are better than others at celebration moments, but we can all train ourselves to see potential reasons to celebrate. Some are obvious and some could easily go unnoticed. Here are some ideas:

Good grades

Yard work effectively done

Problem solving

A project completed

Dad's or Mom's business success

New friendships

A letter from a friend

A book read

An answer to prayer

A good conversation

A healed relationship

A debt paid

A raise in salary

A compliment

Acceptance into college

A milestone

A phone call or email from a distant friend

A vacation planned

A monkey off the back

In addition to the above list are the more obvious—though often overlooked—celebrations of special days, anniversaries, national and religious holidays. It seems pitiful to me that a school system will give children a vacation day and families don't take the time to celebrate. I am not commissioned by Hallmark to make this comment, but we need to get better at celebrating holidays and significant days each year, such as:

Mother's Day
Father's Day
Christmas
Easter
Thanksgiving
Independence Day
Rosh Hashanah
Birthdays
Wedding anniversaries (of parents and grandparents)
Anniversaries of moving into your home
Spiritual birthdays and rebirth days
Baptism
Graduation

My maternal grandmother was a party waiting to happen. She was also the most generous person I have ever known. She was a televangelist's dream come true. Every solicitous letter she ever received was answered with some monetary response. And, much to my joy and benefit, she was my grandmother.

Every letter she sent me contained a little "bubble gum money." You can be sure I opened each one with eager anticipation. Every weekend or overnight visit to her house included a sequence of traditional celebrations, including card games, a few favorite TV programs, a bubble bath, a make-your-own banana split with as many toppings as Baskin-Robbins, and a children's orange-flavored Bayer aspirin before bedtime just for good measure.

I guess her influence rubbed off on my mother, because our family enjoyed nearly continuous celebrations as well. Every evening before dinner, we had a dry happy hour when we sat around, munched peanuts and pretzels, drank Cokes, and debriefed the day. You could say that we looked for excuses to celebrate. My mom lived by the motto, "Give honor where honor is due."

We frequently had guests in our home who would stimulate conversation and enrich our family life. On birthdays, not only did we sing the traditional birthday tune while serving a candle-topped cake, we added a brief, though endearing, little refrain on the end of the song. To my knowledge this habit is uniquely Hartley in origin. It always added an element of family identity and joy to each birthday celebration.

In studying dysfunctional families, researchers have found that one of their most glaring characteristics is the inability to celebrate. For dysfunctional families, weddings, birthdays, and other celebrative moments degenerate into interpersonal disasters. Instead of joy and laughter, they are typified by anger, arguments, yelling, embarrassments, hurts, and alienation. Unhealthy families are unable to enjoy the celebrations of I-like-you households.

Building Block 2: Hobbies

A while ago, when I wanted to please my wife, I attended a craft show with her. Since I wasn't that interested in the crafts, I spent most of my time observing the crowd. I was struck by how friendly and happy they seemed. It was a racially, economically, and socially mixed group of people who seemed bright, agreeable, and creative. I came to the conclusion that hobby people are healthier than the general population.

I-like-you families often enjoy doing hobbies together or at least they applaud the personal hobbies of each individual member. These activities can include virtually any area of shared interest.

- Collections—baseball cards, insects, logo golf balls, Thomas Kinkade paintings, bells, thimbles, match pads, license plates, seashells, model airplanes
- Crafts—woodworking, carpentry, sewing, knitting, quilting, needlepoint, shell crafts
- Trades—auto mechanics, plumbing, electrical, computer
- Reading—novels, history, research, classics, poetry, fiction
- Music—classical, gospel, R&B, jazz, blues, heavy metal, rap
- Drama—Shakespeare, Early American, Modern
- Movies—cinematography, filmmaking

Building Block 3: Traditions

Celebrations quickly become traditions. Our daughter, Andrea, has a theory about family traditions: "It's not a tradition until we do it three years in a row. That gives us two tries to see if we like it enough to officially make it a tradition."

Every family needs to carve their own path and establish their own traditions. Virtually anything can become a tradition, as long as your family buys into it. (Remember, three years in a row, and you have established a tradition!) Keep in mind, however, that one family's tradition can be another family's drag. Here are some ideas:

Game Traditions—after-dinner game of marbles, darts, Sega, Ping-Pong; weekend tennis, golf, or other sport; once-a-year outing to a major sports event, such as the Masters golf tournament or a game at Yankee Stadium.

Special-Day Traditions—family birthdays, graduation days, anniversaries, Fourth of July with the neighbors, after-holiday open house on January 1.

Religious Holiday Traditions—Don't just patronize religious holidays by showing up for church. Get creative. Have your neighbors in and ask them about their traditional celebration of a particular religious day. Show the *Jesus* film and then talk about it. At Christmas, invite the neighbor kids in for Jesus' birthday party.

Heritage Traditions—Celebrating the birthdays of family matriarchs and patriarchs, even after they are gone, can be healthy. (Why not? If you celebrate Martin Luther King Jr. Day, Columbus Day, and Presidents' Day, why not celebrate Grandma's birthday?) Celebrate spiritual rebirth days; celebrate major family events, such as grandparents' wedding anniversary.

Recipe Traditions—favorite chocolate sauce, cakes, pies, homemade ice cream, spaghetti sauce, pizza; hand-me-down recipes for Christmas cookies; family members' favorite meals.

Hobby Traditions—Every summer rebuild a car; every Christmas go snow skiing; every spring replant your vegetable garden together; every weekend attend a baseball card trade show; every so often work on your doll, stamp, coin, arrowhead, or decal collection.

Every tradition is like a cord that binds the family closer together. In fact, traditions that span generations, passed down from parents, grandparents, great-aunts and -uncles, tie us together across the decades and even centuries. Traditions are for people who like each other.

We have heard the old adage, "The family that prays together stays together." We could also say, "The family that plays together stays together."

Building Block 4: Vacation

I-like-you families vacation together. Life is not a vacation, and we shouldn't live for vacation. Hopefully we enjoy our daily routine—including our personal and our professional life. Yet vacations sure make life more fun. They provide an important break, allowing us time to reflect, process, recharge, and reconnect with the most important people in our lives.

I work hard; I play hard; I vacation hard. Being a pastor requires me to invest most weekends and virtually every holiday in my work. For this reason, I do my best to plan and pull off a few meaningful and memorable vacations throughout the year. Some are low budget, some are more expensive, but all are fun.

Without a doubt, our favorite annual vacation spot has become South Seas Plantation off the west coast of south Florida at Fort Myers, thirteen miles out into the Gulf of Mexico on the sheller's paradise—Captiva Island. Our immediate and extended family loves that week. At last count we have thirty-five traditions that come together during those seven days. That may seem like an exhausting list, but we enjoy every minute of it. It's a blast! We each go at our own pace. We sleep plenty and return home refreshed—believe it or not.

Though this may be similar to boring you with family movies, let me share our list of vacation traditions at South Seas:

1. Take the kids out of school by noon on Friday (a tradition the kids love)!
2. Stop at Steak n Shake somewhere along I-75 south.
3. Check into the hotel by 5:00 P.M.
4. Unload by 5:30.
5. Play free golf (usually nine holes) by 6:00.
6. Dinner at Capt'n Al's dockside restaurant at 8:00.
7. Watch Braves baseball games—often the World Series!
8. Shelling contest begins the first morning.
9. The island run (4.2 miles literally from one end of the island to the other).
10. Sand sculpture competition.
11. Floating the pass (riding on inner tubes along the current flowing between the two islands—dangerous but definitely adventurous!).
12. Uncle Bob's ice cream.
13. Beachside worship on Sunday morning.
14. Tennis round-robin, called the "Roseated Spoonbill Invitational," with our own engraved plaque.
15. The evening seafood buffet—local restaurant.
16. "Mushy-Gushy" Islands—shelling on mud flats.
17. Seining—catching live shrimp, sea horses, blowfish, and even an occasional stingray in a dragnet while walking in water up to our armpits.
18. Ben and Jerry's ice cream fest.
19. Bubble bread—a one-of-a-kind dinner roll made with seven cheeses.
20. Diving for sand dollars.
21. Bike riding.
22. Evening fruit smoothies.
23. My dad's birthday—celebrated this week every year with hats, cards, and gifts.

24. Favorite traditional outfits—Atlanta Braves T-shirts and golf shirts from the local links.
25. Trolley rides—complimentary every fifteen minutes.
26. Poolside lounging.
27. Salmon bagels—my personal favorite vacation lunch.
28. Mama Rosa's pizza—the best this side of Rome and Venice!
29. Family Bible reading.
30. Late-night talks out under the stars.
31. Wiffle ball, Frisbee, boccie ball, and football on the beach.
32. Watching the sunset.
33. Nature walks.
34. T-dock fishing.
35. Sea-dooing.

I may have missed a few, but that covers most of them. You certainly get a feel for our vacation time. More important, I hope you can feel the fun we have together. Vacationing together is a central part of normal I-like-you family life.

Building Block 5: Wholesome Humor

Healthy people laugh and healthy families laugh together. They encourage laughter. They look for laughter. Wholesome, clean humor is good for the soul. Dr. Elizabeth Stanley, professor at Arizona State University, extensively surveyed eleven- to sixteen-year-old students and their home life. She concluded, "Parents who joke in a light-hearted fashion during tense or stressful situations . . . may make their adolescents feel more comfortable and accepted, less anxious, and more willing to communicate in a positive manner."

We might think some families are just humorous families and some families are not, but that is normally not the case.

Most families have a comedian-in-residence—someone, who, if given permission and a little encouragement, will be a source of joy and laughter for others in the house. Each home is gifted with its own variety of humor, wit, and healthy folly. When humor is affirmed and encouraged, it will normally blossom and grow quite nicely in virtually every family.

As a professional cartoonist who drew Spiderman, the Hulk, Archie and Jughead, and a host of other cartoon characters, my dad was our comic-in-residence. When my friends came over, my dad was able to tell a joke on virtually any subject. We'd say "cat" and he'd tell a cat joke, or "school" and he'd tell school jokes.

Our youngest son, Andrew, has inherited his grandfather's humor. His teachers at school are already well aware of his prowess. He is earning himself quite a reputation as a comic, which he is learning to channel appropriately.

Some families who are unable to identify their comedian-in-residence have purchased humor cassette tapes, movies, joke books, comics, and other sources of humor to take up the slack. When all else fails, laugh at yourself. The best sources of humor are always the real-life events we all face on a daily basis. Virtually all the TV sitcoms over the years have dealt with real-life situations with which we can all identify, and the characters are always able to laugh at themselves. It started with *The Honeymooners* and *I Love Lucy* and continued with *Leave It to Beaver* and *All in the Family* and more recently *Home Improvement, Family Matters,* and *The Cosby Show.*

Put them all together and we should get the message: Don't take yourself too seriously, particularly if you are a parent who feels in over his head. Chill out! Parenting goes better with laughter. The Bible says, "A cheerful heart is good medicine"

(Prov. 17:22). We all need a good swig of parenting cheer. Merriment, games, parties, hilarity, and raucous laughter are all parts of healthy family life.

Don't Choke the Club

I was standing over the ball. "Don't choke the club," my golf coach scolded me.

"What do you mean, 'don't choke the club'?" I asked, somewhat insecure and somewhat embarrassed.

"You are holding the club too tightly. Look at the flex in your forearm. You are choking the club. It can't swing if you can't feel it move in your hand a little in your back swing." He was beginning to make sense, but he didn't let it drop.

"Address the ball again." I did. "Look at your forearms; they are still flexed. You are not playing baseball. This is golf. You need to hold the club loosely." I told him I understood, but he still pursued it.

"You want the club to swing, don't you? That means it can't be tight. Just think of a swing set. The swing is suspended by rope or chain, not by a stiff shaft. Similarly, if you want that club to swing freely the way it's supposed to swing, you need to lighten up."

Again I assured my instructor the point had sunk in, but he still wouldn't drop it. To add one more piece of information that would clinch his case in my mind forever, he added, "And, Fred, it will add fifty yards to your drive without even moving your arms any faster." That was all I needed to hear. And he was right. Distance is not determined by arm speed or hand speed but rather by club head speed. And club head speed is largely determined by a single principle: Don't choke the club; let it swing itself. It works in golf and it works in parenting.

We all know that parenting is hands-on. From the moment we hold our daughter in the delivery room until we hug her at her wedding and beyond, hands play a strategic role, particularly in communicating affection. Wise parents know when to be hands-on and when to practice quick release. They know when to bring the chicks under their wings and when to nudge them out of the nest. When we practice "don't choke the club" with our daughter, we are saying to her, "I like you; I trust you; I empower you to be you. I will influence you—that is my role as your parent—but I won't fight you or force you. I want you to swing free, to be used to your fullest potential." It says to our son, "You are your own man, a good man. I respect you for who you are. I have confidence in you. I want you to know I will always be here for you, but I can't make all your decisions for you. I simply want to coach you to make good choices."

There is a delicate balance that parents have to try to keep if they want to raise healthy, self-confident children. That's the balance between holding our children lightly, so they can each become their own person, while letting them know how much they mean to us.

All children love to make an impact on their parents. They love to get a laugh, a compliment, a turn of the head, anything. Have you ever played the game with your toddler in which you make a noise or a comical gesture at her cue? You might make a gong sound when she touches your nose, shake your head wildly when she pulls your ear, jump up and down when she holds on to your finger, or wave your arms hilariously when she grabs your foot. Watching my kids belly laugh until they could hardly draw breath as my dad overresponded to such stimuli taught me volumes about parenting.

Our child needs to know that what he does affects us. He needs to know that when he hurts, we hurt, and when he celebrates, we celebrate. When he cracks a joke, we laugh. When he asks deep questions, groping for our honest answers, we are groping with him. When he pursues an area of interest, we honor that interest and when possible join in his pursuit. But our child also needs to know that we can't live his life for him. And as we gradually let go, he will test his own wings and find they are strong enough and he can fly.

Depressurizing the Cabin

The human spirit is made to withstand tremendous amounts of stress and pressure. We endure time pressure, peer pressure, financial pressure, scheduling pressure, relational pressure, and health pressure. Stress is a staple of life in the twenty-first century. To survive the pressure against the family, cope with the stress, and protect the I-like-you family atmosphere, we need to learn how to depressurize the cabin.

The most helpful time management book I have ever read is *Adrenaline and Stress* by Dr. Archibald Hart.[2] In it he tells about *eustress*, which is the positive stress of life in contrast to *distress*, which is the negative, draining, life-sapping stress. He points out that a rubber band is made to stretch, but if it remains stretched, it will oxidize, lose all its elasticity, and eventually disintegrate. Any home that undergoes extended stress will eventually lose its elasticity, its humor, and its ability to laugh at itself and will forfeit its I-like-you atmosphere. When that goes, it won't be long before the family will show signs of the early stages of disintegration. We laugh less and we grip the club too tightly. Our kids feel the pressure. It's too easy for life to become stale, brittle, rigid, and boring.

One way for a family to depressurize the cabin is to have a family night, when you spend the evening together playing games and talking. For some families, though, game night can become hard core, trash-talking, and downright dirty. Competition is good, but intense competition can become ruthless and stressful. It can be characterized by anger, rage, jealousy, spite, revenge, and animosity. Ask yourself, *Do our family games unify or polarize? Do they end with relationships deepened or challenged? Do they invigorate or deflate?* It's usually not difficult to discern the difference.

What is the solution to the challenge of juggling family priorities in our day-to-day stressful life? Return immediately to the five building blocks of healthy, I-like-you families— celebration, hobbies, traditions, vacation, and wholesome humor. Pick them up; dust them off. Take the first logical step for reintroducing at least one of these into your family life. Set your sights on doing your part to provide your spouse and your child with an I-like-you home environment.

Here is a summary of the characteristics of I-like-you families:

- I-like-you families have fun together.
- They value every member as a contributing member.
- They enjoy a good belly laugh together.
- They carry on traditions.
- They so enjoy each other, they invest money in taking vacations together.
- They receive from each other.
- They allow every member's fingerprints to leave a lasting impression.
- I-like-you families intentionally monitor their cabin pressure and know how to blow off steam.
- I-like-you parents don't take themselves too seriously.

A Window into My Child's Heart:
Feeling Treasured

I really love my dad. We are really tight. He and I do this thing with our heads. At special times when my dad wants me to know how much he loves me, he comes up to me, presses his forehead against my forehead real hard, and rubs it back and forth real hard. It might sound funny or odd, but it's really not. To me it is special. For some reason, I am the only one in my family he does that with. I guess I'm the only person in the world he does that with. I guess that's why it is so special.

Andrew Hartley, age fourteen

5

I Love You

I allowed my ministry to get ahead of my family.

John Perkins

Of all powers, love is the most powerful and the most powerless. It is the most powerful because it alone can conquer that final and most impregnable stronghold which is the human heart. It is the most powerless because it can do nothing except by consent.

Frederick Buechner

As I boarded the empty Hyatt Hotel elevator on the twenty-second floor, I wondered how many stops it would make on the way down to the lobby. As the elevator approached the tenth floor, the bell rang, the car slowed down, and the door slid open revealing one of the most comical portraits of modern-day parenting overload I have ever seen.

There stood a dad and his wide-eyed preschool son looking like they were posing for a Norman Rockwell painting. The father was thirty-something, tall and buff, but no match for his overstuffed bags. Over one shoulder hung a garment bag crammed with more clothes than it was designed to carry. Over the other shoulder were slung both his laptop and his son's book bag. One hand grasped a full-size Igloo cooler and the other clutched the largest suitcase American Tourister has ever created. Under each arm he held an oversized duffle bag. He looked more like a pack mule than a man.

As he made his way across the threshold and onto the elevator, he took short choppy steps reminding me of an Olympian weightlifter staggering under free weights. His face was a shade of red somewhere between raspberry and eggplant. "Would you please push Lobby for us?" he grunted. By way of apology—as if I needed an explanation—he added the obvious, "I can't read the button."

I smiled, "No problem." I had everything I could do to hold back my laughter.

On the way down I noticed something I had initially missed. The Igloo cooler was being held by only four fingers; the pinky on the left hand was held straight out and gripped firmly by his son. And only three fingers of his right hand were clutching the super-sized suitcase. Between his thumb and forefinger, he gently pinched his son's balsa biplane, undoubtedly the boy's pride and joy.

My eyes flashed back and forth between the pinky gripped by his son and the balsa model plane in the other hand. The contrast between the brute strength and a gentle touch paints a mural of modern-day life—the tough and the tender, the broad shoulder and the sensitive spirit. There was something noble about this man's determination and his do-what-it-takes effort. I admired his strength and resolve and his willingness to, at the last minute, find two more fingers to carry his son's balsa plane. I admired as well the extended finger for his son's security. Yet at the same time I was concerned. The portrait brings a sober warning.

I couldn't help but say to myself, *If this is what it takes to parent in the twenty-first century, no wonder many of us are exhausted or feeling like failures. Most of us have too many weights, too much responsibility. We're shouldering loads that are unrealistic, inhumane. We're trying to carry the weight of the world and at the same time gently cradle the cherished areas of our kids' lives.*

The picture of the balsa plane—so vulnerable, so fragile, so breakable—is a picture of why our efforts at affection are often so inadequate. We face unrealistic demands and are required to carry loads that seem unfathomably heavy. If we are not careful, we as parents will move from being people to becoming beasts of burden. There are too many demands strapped to our shoulders. The time pressures and scheduling challenges are too much to handle and they leave us with little more to offer our children than the tip of our pinky to grab on to as we shuffle along through life.

It's hard to say "I love you" when our blood pressure is up and we're staggering under inhumane pressures. It's hard to communicate affection when we are preoccupied with too many other demands. Affection is often the first virtue to be sacrificed when family life hits the survival mode.

As parents, we want to give priority to "I love you." Usually we do not fail in this area for lack of good intentions. We know our son longs for more than our pinky, and his balsa dreams require forethought, not afterthought. One thing for sure, he needs more from us than a pinkyful of affection. In this chapter we want to learn how to throw our arms around our sons and daughters and how to fully embrace and cheer for their dreams.

Balsa Parenting

Whether the balsa biplane made it home in one piece or it snapped en route is not the critical issue. What is vital, however, is whether that man's temper snapped, breaking his son's spirit, or were they able to get through the day with their ability to respect each other still intact? When we allow too little margin for our child's life, it is all too easy to sacrifice our relationship with him or her.

Balsa moments are some of the most memorable moments of parenting. They are the creative, tender, wonder-filled, tearful, joyful moments that we experience with our children all along the way:

- when their dog dies
- when they hit the home run
- their first day of kindergarten
- when they forget their lines in the school play
- when your daughter finds out she is pregnant
- when you get a call from the principal's office and learn your son was caught cheating
- the first day she drives the car out of the driveway
- their last day of high school
- during the process of selecting and applying to college
- their first day of college
- when our college student selects a major

- the day you find a bag of marijuana in his dresser
- when you learn she broke up with her boyfriend
- every post-college dating relationship that quickly becomes a potential spouse

I want you to look at the balsa you hold between your fingers right now. You need to realize it won't be there forever. In fact it won't be long before you will wish you had these balsa moments back again. They are fragile, tender, impressionable. They are dreams, identity-shaping moments. They require great respect, care, and intentionality. And if you are not careful, you can crush something highly significant without even paying any attention. Every balsa moment is an opportunity to say to our child, "I love you! Perhaps better than anyone in the world, I know and respect what you are going through right now, and I am here for you with a tender and kind touch."

I love you. There are no more familiar words in the English language, not in any language. There are no more powerful, influential words. "I love you" breathes meaning, dignity, worth, and significance into any life. They are the oxygen of the soul-blood.

When Father God spoke them to his spittin' image Son, the Son's ears tingled. His head turned. He stopped in his tracks. His eyes moistened. He wanted to be sure he heard correctly. A smile lifted from the corner of his lips. He swallowed hard. He breathed in those words deeply as they echoed through the four chambers of his heart. They pressed into his muscle tissue deeper than any massage.

"I love you." Certainly, at midlife, Jesus had heard these words before. He had heard them from Father God, but he needed to hear them once again. Like checking our watch periodically on the way to an appointment to make sure we're on time, those words were reaffirming, refreshing, reassuring, especially for Jesus, when he seemed to be such a long way from home.

The Father wanted his Good Buddy to know he had his eye on him. He wanted Jesus to live in the constant awareness of his love and favor. He didn't want any misgivings, any feelings of insecurity, doubt, or distance to slip in. He wanted his Son to enjoy the strength and confidence of his affection, to taste again the robust flavor of his devotion, and to get his bearings.

What exactly was God saying to his Son?

I—The eternal I Am—Yahweh—the I was, the I am, the I always will be—the forever now God, your Daddy, the One-on-One relationship we have forever enjoyed and forever will enjoy—as good today as ever.

Love—The real thing, gift love, sacrifice love, eternal love, tough love, Messiah love, giving and forgiving love. This love is the kind you and I have a patent on, not a knock-off, look-alike, phony, generic love. I am talking about the pure, holy, miracle-working, life-transforming, greatest-force-in-the-universe variety of love, the kind I have for the world, which motivated me to send you in the first place. My kind of love is risky, vulnerable, lavish, opulent, and extravagant. It takes a licking but keeps on ticking. It is full of unconditional positive regard and is undeserved, unearned, and unending. My Son, I want you to know I love you so much there is nothing you will ever do to make me love you more. I have incurable love for you. Nothing will ever separate us; neither death nor life, neither angels nor demons, neither the present nor the future, nor anything else in all creation will be able to separate the two of us from our covenant love for each other.

You—You, Jesus, are the apple of my eye, the joy in my heart, the pride of my life. Did you hear me? I said *you,* just you. I'm not talking to that other guy over there; I'm talking just to you, my firstborn, my only begotten, my from-everlasting-to-everlasting. Jesus—there has never been another and there never will be. No one could ever take your place, not even close. Did you hear me? I love *you!* Let it sink into every corpuscle of your body. I love you. Let it rattle around your brain a few thousand times. I want you to marinate in these three words. They are huge. I want my affection for you to fill you with zeal. Don't just take a sip and put this goblet down. I want you to drink this potion to the dregs. I want you to get intoxicated on the fact that your Daddy is head over heels in love with you. I can't get you out of my mind; you are in my hands, my loving hands.

This expression of love is light-years beyond a measly pinkyful of affection; this is a mother lode of affection. This is the kind every child longs for. Needless to say, aspects of this expression of love are uniquely Father God to Son God, and rightly so. However, the vast majority of these words apply to every father-son, father-daughter, mother-son, and mother-daughter relationship. And beyond these words, we want to find our own unique ways to communicate our affection to our unique child.

Believe it or not, your son or daughter is waiting to hear affectionate words from you. This lavish kind of love is a healing ointment that needs to be thoroughly rubbed into the emotional cracks that chafe and bleed. It is impossible to overlove your child. We don't need to put a governor on our love flow and ration it out. We don't need to worry about smothering or spoiling or strangling our child with our love. We won't run out, so we don't need to ration. And it won't spoil him, so there's no reason to withhold it. This is true of affection, as well as acceptance and affirmation. Our child needs all we can give him.

Now, while it is impossible to overlove a child, it's certainly possible to love a child inappropriately. The key is learning his or her love language.

Love Languages

When our child recoils, stiffens, pushes away, wrinkles her nose, and declares, "Oh, yuck, Dad! I hate it when you tell me you love me," or "Mom, get away from me! Don't you ever hug me again in public!" we may wonder what the problem is. It is easy to lose altitude in parental confidence in a hurry. We can quickly conclude our relationship with our child is about to crash and burn. Actually the problem may be as simple as misunderstanding his love language. The key to communicating "I love you" to our child is learning to express it in terms he or she can understand.

Gary Chapman struck a deep chord with his book *The Five Love Languages*. His thesis is that everyone understands love in his or her own unique language. While there are different accents and dialects, there are essentially five basic languages in which people give and receive love. If we want to express love to our son or daughter, it is essential that we know his or her love language. Otherwise, our finest efforts may be entirely ineffective. Chapman's language groupings are straightforward. For the sake of brevity, let's attempt our own Cliff Notes summary.[1]

1. *Words of Affirmation*, expressed either verbally or in writing: "You are special." "I'm so proud of you." "You're so sweet." "I learn a lot from you." "I'd rather spend time with you than anyone else."
2. *Quality Time*, involving extended moments together: sitting, walking, playing, talking, and so on.
3. *Receiving Gifts*, tangible or intangible, such as: flowers, bubble gum, a card, clothes, an afternoon together.
4. *Acts of Service*, such as: cleaning a room, doing laundry, chauffeuring.
5. *Physical Touch*, such as: a hug, a kiss, a pat on the back.

If your daughter's love language is receiving gifts and you are smothering her with words of affection, she may not get the message. You might as well be speaking Swahili. If your son's love language is quality time and you lavish him with physical touch, you could well be driving him from you rather than drawing him alongside.

If you find these love languages more confusing than helpful, don't get bogged down. The essence of parenting is to keep the focus on love, not language. Your son wants to know he is loved regardless of the language he speaks. Your daughter wants to feel your affection; she doesn't expect you to be a skilled linguist. If you are confused, try different love languages to see which one elicits the most favorable response. Keep the focus on your child and your love for him or her by reminding yourself:

1. I speak these words of affirmation because I love you.
2. I spend quality time with you because I love you.
3. I give you these gifts because I love you.

4. I do these acts of service because I love you.
5. I give you my appropriate physical touch because I love you.

We want to keep the emphasis on the right syllable. The language is not as important as the love. The Bible records an often-used motto: "Love covers over a multitude of sins" (1 Peter 4:8). In parenting lingo that means when your child knows you love him, he will cut you more slack.

Love Holds Homes Together

Love has sticking power. You can walk away from money, buildings, jobs, homes, people, prestige, power, influence—but it's hard to walk away from someone who truly cares. Love that clearly expresses the three core needs of the human spirit—the need for acceptance, the need for affection, and the need for affirmation—is rarely brushed aside and jilted, not for long and not forever.

John Perkins is one of my heroes. He is an African American Christian leader who is transforming urban communities by demonstrating radical Christian love in terms people can understand, and he is personally one of the most loving men I have ever met. I had the opportunity to speak at the Promise Keepers stadium event in Atlanta in 1996, and John introduced me to the group of 62,000 men. John is the father of eight children. He explains that the first four children received quite a bit of attention, but the last four received less as his outside-the-home career activities expanded. Listen to his honest story and feel his pain.

At the holidays one year, my daughter Priscilla and I were cleaning up the kitchen. She began to tell me she felt we had put the ministry ahead of the children and how she didn't know us. There was a lot of truth in what she was saying and I began to weep. She put her hands on mine and said, "But, Daddy, you still have the chance to make it up. You still have us." That was the turning point in my life.[2]

I am drawn to John's life because of his authenticity and vulnerability. Like any achiever, he has felt the tension between his professional life and his private life. And like thousands of other Christian men in the trenches, his legitimately tender and humble heart was able to listen to his daughter's plea. It wasn't easy to receive those words, but he made the necessary adjustments so that he would be able to win not only the urban communities of America but also his own children's hearts. To paraphrase Jesus' words: What does it profit someone to gain the whole world and lose his or her own son or daughter? (see Matt. 16:26).

I love you, John. Thank you for not snapping the balsa spirit of your daughter. Thank you for leading me, leading us all, to make needed adjustments in our careers so that we can communicate to our sons and daughters in no uncertain terms that they are of greater worth to us than our reputation, our agendas, our career, and even our life. There may be no more crystal clear way of saying, "Son, I love you" or, "Daughter, you are my pride and joy." Laying aside the things we value for the sake of our child, who is of far greater value, speaks volumes.

I have a conviction that all children have the right to know that they are more important in the hearts of their parents than just about anything else—certainly more important than their parent's career, reputation, and other personal pursuits. Children intuitively feel the level of worth their parent places on them in direct relationship to how that worth corresponds to their parent's other priorities. When children see their parent place greater importance on personal pursuits than on them, they will be deeply wounded. When, on the other hand, children know they are of much greater worth than personal pursuits, they will have a security, stability, dignity, and self-worth that will deeply bind them in loyalty to their parents. This principle is true for brain surgeons, missionaries, plumbers, and college professors. It's true for any parent. We must be willing to make hard choices that communicate to our sons and daughters our preference, priority, and passion for them.

When Jesus said, "Greater love has no one than this, that he lay down his life for his friends" (John 15:13), he was highlighting this parenting principle.

Bill Bright, founder and president of Campus Crusade, who certainly knows the challenge of juggling family priorities, says:

> Every teen needs a "comfort zone"—a place where he knows he is loved and accepted and appreciated unconditionally, not based on "because" or "if" or "when." . . . The home is the best comfort zone because it is the one place where the teenager is really loved. . . . I tell our sons "I love you" almost every time I see them. One day I said to myself, "Maybe they get tired of hearing me say that." So I asked them, and they both said, "Oh, no." I don't think anyone gets tired of hearing "I love you" if it is genuine.[3]

I have seen that balsa plane a thousand times in my own mental replay. It has become one of my favorite parenting videos. I watch it often just to remind myself how fragile my child's heart is and how fragile her dreams and concerns are.

I don't ever want to break or crack what my children value. I don't want to accumulate so much stuff that what my son or daughter values becomes an afterthought. I don't want my devotion to life's possessions to diminish my ability to tenderly care for and protect the dignity and honor of my children. Not for what they say, not for what they accomplish, but simply for who they are, I want them to know they are loved.

Lessons from Football

The reason *being* precedes and outshines *doing* is that doing is not always possible. Consider the Buoniconti family for example.

Nick Buoniconti played professional football as well as anyone who's ever played the game. With the Miami Dolphins, he competed in two consecutive Super Bowls, including the Super Bowl VII victory that capped the Dolphin's 17-0 season. In fact it was his interception as part of the "no-name defense" that set up the winning touchdown.

The day Buoniconti was inducted into the Pro Football Hall of Fame in Canton, Ohio, he was one of several men to receive the NFL's highest honor. It was, however, the induction speech that drew the loudest applause, not necessarily because Buoniconti deserved it more than Buffalo Bills' coach Marv Levy, Minnesota Vikings' tackle Mark Youngblood, Pittsburgh Steelers' wide receiver Lynn Swann, or the others. The man who spoke had played college football for the Citadel, wearing the same uniform number—eighty-five—that Buoniconti had worn and playing the same position—linebacker. He spoke from a wheelchair to which he has been confined since his paralyzing spinal injury, suffered while playing college football. He is thirty-four-year-old Marc Buoniconti, Nick's son. His compelling, emotional speech brought the fans out of their seats.

"Here I am, one lucky person," he told the spellbound crowd, "a kid who grew up with his hero as his dad." Poignantly, Marc commented to his dad, "This game of football gave you your greatest moments and your greatest sorrow." If there were a hall of fame for fathers, Marc intimated, his dad belonged there too, because of his fight to find a cure for paralysis. "Dad, this is where you excel."

In response Nick recalled the shock and horror of receiving the doctor's phone call breaking the news of his son's paralysis and Nick's resulting feelings of helplessness, guilt, and instant determination to do whatever was possible to find help for his son. Pointing to his cherished, ever-present Super Bowl ring, he quickly commented, "I'd trade this ring and all my individual honors if one thing can happen in my lifetime. Marc dreams to someday walk. As his father, I'd like nothing more than to walk by his side." He confidently added, "We will find a cure for paralysis."[4]

Did you hear that? Essentially, Nick Buoniconti said that he would trade his career for his son. Every daughter and son wants to hear those words. They need to hear those words. They deserve to hear those words. When Marc's spinal cord snapped like balsa, his dad didn't allow his son's spirit to snap. Like a good dad, he quickly, instinctively came alongside to shower his son with unconditional love, respect, and favor.

When it comes to your kids, love them lavishly, liberally, wastefully, extravagantly. Love them in a language they can understand. Love them thoroughly. Love them anyway. Love them always—not for what they do but because of who they are and whose they are. And make the most of those balsa moments.

Listen to the emphasis C. S. Lewis puts on affection: "We can say anything to one another. The truth behind this is that Affection at its best wishes to say whatever Affection at its best wishes to say, regardless of the rules that govern public courtesy; for Affection at its best wishes neither to wound nor to humiliate nor to domineer."[5]

Here is a summary of the characteristics of I-love-you families:

- I-love-you families celebrate together and cry together.
- They celebrate a child's wins.
- They cry together over a child's losses.
- Parents handle with care the balsa wood moments.
- They take every opportunity to verbally affirm their child.
- Parents know their child well enough to be certain of his or her love language and dialect.
- I-love-you families touch each other, giving hugs, kisses, pats on the back.
- Parents in I-love-you families are willing to give up time in their busy schedule to invest in their child.

A Window into My Child's Heart: Unconditional Love

I remember standing in the police department one afternoon, wondering, *What have I gotten myself into?* I had
done something that was extremely embarrassing. After
answering a series of questions, I was told to call my
parents. My initial thoughts were, *What are my parents
going to think? How do I tell them?* Immediately my
heart was filled with guilt and shame. I knew I had let
my parents down. When I called and told my dad what
I had done and asked him to come get me, I sensed the
disappointment in his voice.

As my father pulled up to the police station, I wondered, *Will my parents ever forgive me?* I can remember
the silence in the car as my father drove us home. When
we arrived, Dad asked me to meet him in the "discussion" room, and I knew I was in for it.

What happened, though, was not what I expected.
My dad was obviously saddened by my behavior, and
this made me sad. I had never seen him like that before.
He told me that, although he was disappointed in me,

he still loved me. Hearing him say that made me feel better but it kind of broke me at the same time.

Even though Dad was able to handle my misbehavior and forgive me, I knew my life needed a deep change. I recall kneeling with my dad, our faces flat on the cushions of the couch. With tears in my eyes, I thanked the Lord for his all-sufficient grace in allowing me to receive forgiveness for my sins. After a time of groaning in prayer, my dad and I gave each other a big hug.

Fred IV

6

I Love You Anyway

To please God . . . to be a real ingredient in the divine happiness, to be loved by God, not merely pitied, but delighted in as an artist delights in his work, as a father in his son . . . it seems impossible, a weight, a burden of glory which our thoughts can hardly sustain. But so it is!

C. S. Lewis

Hell is the punishment for being unable to love.

Dostoyevsky

Expressing love in terms our child can understand is number one on every parent's job description. This is the single assignment that defines our success. Our son does not really care how much we pay for his basketball shoes, but he cares deeply about how many games we watch him play. Our daughter is not as interested in the number of square feet in our home as she is in how kindly we talk to each other inside it. We have already considered I-love-you-*because* parenting. This is where we all begin. However, the longer I parent, the more I realize that this level of love has severe limitations. Sooner or later I-love-you-*because* parenting will need to pass the baton to I-love-you-*anyway* parenting.

Our daughter, our only daughter, Andrea, is a fierce competitor. She played four years of high school varsity basketball with the eye of the tiger. As an inside post player, she graduated with the most rebounds for either the girls or the boys varsity teams. Her senior year, when her team was scheduled to play their arch rival from the other side of Atlanta, whom they had never beaten, her brother came home from college to watch.

What a battle! We were leading the entire game, and Andrea played every second. She was making shots she had no right even taking. She shot from the top of the key, from the three-point line, even from half court, and she sunk them! At first, I would mumble under my breath from the stands, "Oh, no, don't take that shot!" Then a split second later—swoosh! "Nice shot! Nice shot!" I screamed.

Our fans looked up at Sherry and me standing behind them in the bleachers, then to the team on the floor. Smiles were big and our fingers were crossed. In the fourth period the momentum shifted. The margin of our lead began to diminish, and the opposing team inched ever closer. With only a few seconds to go, our rivals sank the winning shot. "AAAGGH-HHH!" Our bleachers were silent; we all shook our heads in disbelief. Some looked at Sherry and me with heads down, speechless. She was crying.

Then we heard a gasp rise from the people in our bleachers. Sherry tugged my arm, "Oh, honey, look!" Out on the middle of the floor stood our son—our firstborn—with his arms wrapped tightly around his sweat-drenched sister. The shoulders of both of them were heaving as they sobbed together on center court.

That is a snapshot no one will ever remove from the scrapbook of my Hartley family memories. What a picture of unconditional affection! Andrea's team may have lost the game, but that was a big win for our family. What made the biggest impression on me was the fact that many brothers would have distanced themselves from their sister at that moment. Forget the fact that she played a great game or that she had done her best. She lost. And for that reason alone, lesser men would have silently slipped away, but not Fred. He didn't see a loser; he saw a hurting sister who left her heart and soul on the court that night. Every instinct in his body moved him to walk out and wrap his love around her vulnerable dignity and hold her tight. His instincts served him well. Who knows what he verbalized to his sis in that tender moment. One thing for sure, what he did spoke volumes. Fred demonstrated love that night on center court, and everyone knew it. It was the I-love-you-anyway variety.

- I-love-you-anyway love protects people's dignity and self-worth, especially when they are vulnerable and exposed.
- I-love-you-anyway love steps in when others step out.
- I-love-you-anyway love is sensitive and compassionate.

One of the greatest expressions of pure love is found in the Bible:

Love is patient, love is kind. It does not envy, it does not boast, it is not proud. It is not rude, it is not self-seeking, it is not easily angered, it keeps no record of wrongs.

Love does not delight in evil but rejoices with the truth.
It always protects, always trusts, always hopes, always
perseveres. Love never fails.

1 Corinthians 13:4–8a

When the Stakes Are Higher

Losing a basketball game is one thing, but what do we do
when the stakes are higher? What do we do when our daughter loses her virginity, when our son loses his integrity, when
our family loses its reputation? What does love do when our
son or daughter loses something of much greater value than
an athletic contest?

How do you handle your child's losses—his moral losses
or spiritual losses? How do you respond to the knuckle-headed
decisions your child makes? What about his stubborn, rebellious, defiant, perhaps illegal behavior? When you observe
from the parenting bleachers the shattered ego of your child
lying in pieces on the floor, how do you respond? How should
you respond?

These questions are honest and highly relevant. When we
stand next to our child in the principal's office, the medical
clinic, the emergency room, or behind bars, the undergirding
principle is I-love-you-anyway. It says, I love you, and I will
always love you, no matter what you do. You will always
be my daughter. You will always have my last name. I will
never disown you or be ashamed of you or cut you off from
my love. My love for you is not for sale. It is unconditional.
This variety of love is better than I-love-you-because. This
kind is I-love-you-anyway.

We have a God who loves us like that. We have a God who
walks out of the bleachers, walks right out into the middle of

the court when we feel like losers. He picks us up. He embraces us. When people may silently slip away and distance themselves, we have a big brother, Jesus, who wraps his loving arms around us and holds us close. He is a man of sorrows and knows how to weep with us. When we win, he loves to cheer and celebrate with us in the locker room after the game, and when we lose, he loves us anyway. When our self-esteem is intact, he loves us, and when it has shattered in the middle of the court, he loves us.

I-Love-You-Anyway Moments

Family life is full of opportunities to say, "I love you because." If you miss one today, there will always be more tomorrow. I-love-you-anyway moments, however, are far less common. If you miss an I-love-you-anyway moment, you may miss an opportunity of a lifetime. By nature, these moments are extremely volatile, infrequent, and high-risk. They sneak up on us unannounced and arrive when we least expect them. We should be looking for them, so that we don't miss these high-impact opportunities to express our love to our child. As we will discover, there are five distinct I-love-you-anyway moments all parents can expect to encounter.

Boundary Lines

The biggest little word in a parent's vocabulary is *no*. Why is that tiny two-letter exclamation so difficult to get out of our throats? Part of the reason is we forget that disciplinary boundary lines are an essential part of loving our children.

Sally is an overextended single mom. I was exhausted listening to her describe her schedule. She is a full-time legal secretary, sixth-grade room mother, chauffeur for her daughter's softball team and her son's soccer team, and Sunday school teacher. She just enrolled in an aerobics class, not to mention a half dozen other extracurricular activities. I couldn't resist asking her point-blank, "Why did you get yourself in way over your head?"

She looked at me and, with a blank look on her face, slowly mouthed the words, "I can't say no." Then she elaborated, "I have always had difficulty saying no. My ex seems to give my children everything. I don't want to look like the bad guy. I want my kids to like me. I want to be their friend. I am so afraid of losing them. And I admit, the older they are the worse it gets. First it was bedtime, then ice cream, then food and diet, homework, respect, manners, you name it. I can't say no. Sure, my schedule is out of control, but, even worse, my home is out of control!"

By now in our conversation, I was committed to offering Sally whatever relief I could give her. "Sally, do you love your children?" I asked.

"Oh, yes!" She assured me. "That's exactly my problem. I want them to know that I love them." After a long, thoughtful pause, she added, "I just don't know how to express it."

Sally's story may be your story. In a sense it is every parent's story, particularly those who have more gum than they can chew. How do we demonstrate our love for our child? Beyond that, how do we demonstrate I-love-you-anyway love?

What Sally and I talked about that afternoon was enlightening and pivotal to her. A few months later she told me that it was a turning point not only in her home life but in her heart life. We talked about the importance of boundary lines in a child's life and how we parents must have the courage to say no at the appropriate times.

I said to her, "Sally, *no* is one of the most loving words in a parent's vocabulary." I asked her a few rhetorical questions. "If you saw your daughter about to run out into the street in front of an oncoming car, would you shout a loud, forceful, commanding *no*?" She nodded in the affirmative. "If you saw her standing in front of an open cupboard, about to take a drink out of a bottle of cleaner, would you cry out with a sharp and immediate *no*?" A slight smile rose from the corners of her lips.

"Sally," I continued, "loving boundary lines are also appropriate for bedtimes and food and friends and morals and values. And, Sally, you are parent first, friend second. Your I-like-you relationship will only flow out of your I-love-you relationship. Even if it means you temporarily risk your children's disfavor, in the long run you will win their respect. Just keep in mind at all times, *I am showing them love by saying no. I owe them boundary lines—loving boundary lines.* This is one of the most taxing aspects of parenting. Strong, virtuous children are raised by strong, virtuous parents who hold firmly to boundary lines."

The times when we establish boundary lines are I-love-you-anyway moments—make-it-or-break-it moments—in family life. In one way or another, every time we face the need to set boundary lines, we need to be able to look our son squarely in the eye and say, "I am setting this boundary line because I love you."

Whether we admit it or not, every child is born a con artist. I've never met an exception. All children know how to apply the pressure. They are innately adept at manipulation, intimidation, nagging, pestering, conning, and playing one against another and both ends against the middle. They can plead their case like an F. Lee Bailey, a Johnny Cochran, or any other high-priced attorney. These kids are good. They know how to attack us when we are vulnerable, when our defenses are down, when we least expect it. They don't need a class, seminar, or instructional video series to learn these skills. They are instinctive, intuitive. To call them smart is an understatement. They are brilliant! And they know just how to push, apply pressure, and turn up the heat. Little did we know while making love with our honey and conceiving our little darling and bringing the little bundle of joy home from the hospital that behind those fat cheeks and innocent smile lurked a world-class con artist. And what makes matters worse is that no one warned us. No one told us we would be raising wheelers and dealers. Few of us realized that we would be responsible to purge the folly pent up in their bones.

Have you ever watched preschool toddlers play together? Let me rephrase that. Have you ever seen preschool toddlers fight over the same toys, slap for the same sandbox space, throw a tantrum until they are literally blue in the face because they couldn't attack with murderous hatred in their eyes another kid who got to the Big Wheel first? I have. These observations have strengthened my parenting courage and enabled me to see the love behind placing limitations on my children. It has given me the intestinal fortitude needed to say one of the biggest words in a parent's vocabulary— no! When we pull splinters from a child's foot, she rarely expresses her appreciation. Usually the child screams and kicks and fights us tooth and nail. It's not until the splinter is gone and things calm down that she realizes that we have actually done her a favor.

Kids cry when they get shots, but, because the benefit of the injection exceeds the momentary sting, we don't back down. We don't wait indecisively to make the appointment until they concur with our decision. We choose what is good for them, endure the hollering, take them home, and enjoy the peace of mind that comes when we know we've done what is best. We made a loving choice that temporarily seemed to them like treason. The sting from the syringe was actually a sting of love.

Discipline is a lot like a measles shot. In reality, love and discipline go hand in hand. If we can't discipline, we really don't love. Knowing this, we can understand that love and discipline are wired together. A dad or mom needs to be able to say, bold-eyed and broad-shouldered, to the child, "I love you enough to say no once in a while. I love you enough to not give you everything you beg me for. I love you so much I can't let you have your way this time. The best way I can express my love to you right now is to refuse to let you talk me into this one." Call it hard-nosed; call it tough love; it is essential for effective parenting.

Negotiation

It is vital that we choose our boundary lines wisely. If we waffle back and forth indecisively, we will lose our children's respect and heighten their frustration and insecurity. However, it is equally important to allow flexibility on issues of less consequence.

During my childhood, my parents would normally permit negotiation. I enjoyed the ability to make my appeals and plead my case. They were often flexible and willing to negotiate curfews, activities, purchases, and other issues. On certain items, however, they would reach a point where they would invoke the "absolute no" or "absolute yes" with which there was no room for appeal. All wiggle room was now removed, and I might as well save my breath. The matter was settled. Case closed.

At the time, I didn't realize just how wise this parenting technique really was. Looking back I can see that it achieves a host of positive results.

- It teaches the child to think for himself, specifically to think about the principle behind the rule in question.
- It teaches the child to make an appropriate appeal and to negotiate creatively.
- It provides a healthy context for animated, lively discussion.
- It gives the parents a heart. Rather than every rule being set in stone, it enables the child to watch the parent think out loud and possibly even be talked out of something. (That is always a delightful prospect!)
- It gives the parent the opportunity to discuss the *why*, not just the *what*, to discuss the principle behind the policy. Parenting without principles is doomed to failure. If children are given only policy and are never given the rationale for the principle that undergirds the policy, a tragic process often develops during the college years. Nearly all college students will crumple up those policies and toss them in the nearest dumpster. Parents who teach principles, however, often observe that the child has a greater ownership of those principles during her college years.

Here are some examples of when an absolute no is appropriate:

- Absolutely no members of the opposite sex in the house when we are not home.
- Absolutely no drinking and driving.
- Absolutely no premarital sexual activity while you are living under our roof.
- Absolutely no stealing money from my wallet.

Here are some examples of when an absolute yes is appropriate:

- Yes, you must treat your mother with respect.
- Yes, you must do certain chores around the house.
- Yes, you must tell the truth.
- Yes, you must attend one worship service a week while you are living at home.

Here are some possible areas of flexibility:

- weekend bedtime
- weekend curfew
- choice of music
- summer job
- investment or expenditure of discretionary money
- choice of friends
- choice of faith
- extracurricular activities

The older the child gets, the more important it is for the parent to transfer the establishment of boundaries to the child. This responsibility is transferred gradually and virtually continuously from birth to adulthood.

It's tragic that too many parents miss this concept altogether. They miss the opportunities to transfer the setting of boundaries to their child during his high school years, so that when they leave their child at college, he is an accident waiting to happen. The child's rebellion is ready to erupt like a volcano at the first opportunity. Chuck Swindoll has perceptively said:

Parents make a big mistake when they don't start affecting their teenagers in a favorable manner from Day One. But they make a bigger mistake—perhaps the biggest—when they discover their dilemma late and become overly zealous to make up for lost time. Wise parents, on the other hand, intentionally begin the process of transferring the boundary line choices early on, so that by the time an independent living arrangement is in place, their child is ready to make the correct moral choices based on the moral principles they have already adopted.[1]

The gift of negotiation is a gift of love. It is an essential part of I-love-you-anyway parenting. Every time we allow negotiation and every time we remove it, by invoking the absolute no and absolute yes, we want to be sure we are clearly communicating, "Son, I am giving you this gift because I love you." "Daughter, I love you enough to allow you to make this choice."

Consequences

When a boundary line that has been established by the absolute no or yes is violated, it requires some sort of consequence or punishment. Just as the boundary lines are appropriate and loving, so are the consequences. Though we always want to do what we can to avoid entering into an adversarial relationship with our son or daughter, and we certainly do not want our parenting to degenerate to resemble the FBI, CIA, or local police, we need to be ready to hold the line. There are times that, for a season, we need to be willing to risk appearing like the enemy.

Consequence (punishment) is tricky. I know of nothing in parenting that requires more creativity, intestinal fortitude, and courage than to stick to our guns and implement consequences. The conflict created by discipline is usually harder on the parents than it is on the child. To take away a child's driver's license or at least suspend his use of the car can exact a huge toll on parents who have enjoyed hanging up their chauffeur's license for a while. Telling a daughter she cannot attend the Saturday night dance because of a broken curfew, moral failure, deception, or dismal grades will truly hurt the parents more than her. These decisions require us to be wise as snakes and gentle as doves. As best we can, we want to be sure the consequence fits the crime and in some way contributes redemptively in teaching and training to benefit our child's future choices. These consequences do not need to always be preestablished or announced in advance, but they certainly should be implied and anticipated.

We don't want to impulsively grab for consequences as discipline any more than we would recklessly grab a loaded gun. Trigger-happy discipline is a killer. It kills our chances to legitimately benefit our child. It kills our rapport. It kills our child's trust in our leadership. It damages our child's ability to make future hard choices on his own. When our child grossly disappoints us and we are forced to resort to discipline for his misbehavior, there are a few vital steps we should take before imposing consequences:

Take a deep breath.

Count to ten—or twenty!

Wait long enough to get your blood pressure down and your anger under control.

Walk around the block.

Buy time. Say something like, "You will need to be punished for this, but I am too upset right now to think clearly. Rather than arbitrarily making a rash decision,

I will tell you tomorrow morning what will be the consequences of your misbehavior."

As difficult or as painful as it may seem, every time we give our child the gift of consequences for his or her misbehavior, we are actually saying, "I love you." All punishment is, thereby, redemptive, never punitive.

Reality

Parents are wired instinctively to put pillows under their children so when they fall, they will land softly. Pillows are a good idea. They work well for gymnasts, wrestlers, and high jumpers. But for healthy childhood formation, particularly during adolescence, parental pillows are out of place because pillows shield our children from reality.

A popular sociological term at the beginning of the twenty-first century is "reality therapy." It refers to the formational need every person has to learn from some of the cruel realities of life, including poverty, violence, addiction, prison, taxes, rent payments, mortgages, and electric and food bills. The welfare system created its own set of problems by giving benefits to people without teaching them responsibility. Consequently it stripped good people of their dignity. Reality therapy gives people the gift of dignity and integrity by enabling them to gain an accurate view of reality.

Reality therapy works for children as well. Here are some examples:

When your child forgets her lunchbox for the fourth day in a row, don't just run it to school. Let her know the next time she will go hungry. She will not die of starvation. You didn't forget your lunch; your child did. You are not a bad parent if you allow your child to learn a valuable lesson. Missing lunch is reality therapy.

Not paying bail to get your son out of jail may be more loving than posting bond.

Telling your new teenage driver that you will pay auto insurance, but, if she gets a ticket, the entire insurance payment becomes hers. The two-hundred-dollar monthly payment is reality therapy.

At whatever age you determine it is appropriate, tell your son to set his own alarm and wake himself in the morning. Let him know that, for the first two weeks, if he forgets, you will wake him up. But from then on, if he doesn't wake up, he misses school. Since the prospect of a day off from school may be more of an incentive than a liability to some students, you may want to drive him to school, but charge a chauffeur fee. The consequences of missing school and the fee are both examples of reality therapy.

Like every good leader, parents are to equip their children with an accurate view of reality. This is true even when reality is not pretty or pleasant. The gift of reality is a gift of love.

At no time do we pay more parenting dues than when we "apply the board of education to the seat of learning" and refuse to compromise, even when it means our child probably won't understand. This is the tough-nosed mom who holds the line, sets the curfew, the boundary lines, the consequences. It's the dad who dares to use the word *no* and holds to certain moral standards based on eternal values and personal convictions.

We can greatly relieve the stress level of discipline in our home if we actually believe that an appropriate act of discipline is in reality an act of love. If we swallow that, we will be like Popeye swallowing spinach—it will boost our inner strength. And if we can help our children swallow it, they will become stronger as well.

Dignity

Each of these I-love-you-anyway opportunities—boundary lines, negotiation, consequences, and reality—contribute to our child's dignity, protection, and enhancement. In that way, they all provide moments to demonstrate our love.

- I love you enough to set boundary lines.
- I love you enough to sometimes negotiate those boundary lines with you.
- I love you enough to set consequences for your inappropriate behavior.
- I love you enough to let you see, taste, and feel reality.

When parental discipline operates in this context, it always raises the dignity level of our home for everyone involved. Where discipline and punishment cross the line—being expressed in anger, pride, or condescension—they strip a son or daughter of his or her self-worth. When the attitude in our voice or the look in our eyes or the words we recklessly use steal the worth of our child, we have dipped beneath the discipline line and moved into destructive behavior.

Destructive discipline, whether verbal or nonverbal, can say things we will one day deeply regret. These include:

- Words spoken in anger, pride, or insensitivity.
- Attitudes of superiority that nonverbally communicate, "You are stupid," "You are a loser," "You will never amount to anything."
- Name calling, such as "jerk" or "idiot."

- Unfair comparisons, such as, "Why can't you be more like your sister?" or "When I was your age, I never . . ."
- Negative characterizations, which, like curses, plant negative thought patterns: "You are a lousy student," "You never get good grades," "You have no musical talent," "You can't hold a job."

The line of demarcation between constructive and destructive discipline is the line of dignity. Our words, our attitudes, our facial countenance, and our actions can communicate respect, honor, and value to our child. At other times they can communicate disrespect, dishonor, and a sense of worthlessness to our child. The critical issue is not what discipline or what boundary line or what consequence we establish. The critical issue is the message our child receives through our discipline. We must ask, am I communicating dignity to my son? Does my daughter feel my utmost respect for her personhood? In the middle of this otherwise loathsome circumstance, how can I restore, establish, protect, and increase my child's sense of dignity?

What makes this an even more critical issue is that often our teenage child will face his moments of moral or ethical failure at the same time he is facing an identity crisis. Already he lacks confidence in who he is and is even less confident of what he is worth. Then, at the same time, he experiments with narcotics or she gets pregnant or he steals a pair of shoes from the department store. It all fits. The last thing our child needs is an angry parent barking out cruel comments, like alcohol being poured into open wounds.

When our daughter stands out in the middle of the basketball court after losing the game, the last thing she needs is a lecture on what she needs to do to win next time. She needs love. It is not I-love-you-because; it is I-love-you-anyway. It is true love, high-respect love, life-transforming love.

C. S. Lewis had a knack for succinctly putting tough issues in terms we can all understand: "The great thing to remember is that, though our feelings come and go, His love for us does not. It is not wearied by our sin, or our indifference; and therefore, it is quite relentless in its determination that we shall be cured of those sins, at whatever cost to us and at whatever cost to Him."[2]

This is the kind of love God has for each of us, and he wants us to experience this kind of radical love in our homes. This is not a pipe dream or religious talk. This revolutionary love is available to every parent. And it is equally available to our child.

Alice Smith, in her book *Beyond the Veil,* tells a dramatic story to vividly demonstrate the life-transforming effect of this kind of unconditional, I-love-you-anyway love.

A story is told about a woman whose face was scarred severely in a fire. Badly disfigured, it was difficult to believe she had once been quite beautiful. She and her husband had a demanding little daughter who was unhappy and embarrassed by the grotesquely scarred face of her mother. With shocking insensitivity, the heartless child reserved all affection from her mother. She refused to be seen with her mother in public and would not bring her friends home to play.

The troubled mother quietly grieved over their relationship while the daughter became more cruel and more distant with age.

Not long after the young woman had gone off to college, her mother became seriously ill and lay dying. The father called their only child to say good-bye to her mother.

Aware of his daughter's obvious anger for being inconvenienced, her father stopped the young woman outside the door of the hospital room. He said, "I think it's about time that you know something. Your mother has always been gracious and understood your feelings about her condition. She knew you were embarrassed to be with her. All these years she has made me promise not to tell you the truth about her scars. Now I think you need to know.

"When you were only six months old, our house caught on fire. You are so pretty, and you look just like your mother once did. She could not bear the thought of losing you. Willing to lay down her life for yours, she broke through the arms of the fire-fighters, entered the burning house, and rescued you. Tears coursed down the melting skin of her face as she emerged from that raging inferno severely burned and forever disfigured. However, your mother was overjoyed that you were safe and unharmed. Maybe now you can understand why she did not want you growing up feeling guilty every time you looked into her marred face."

The heartbroken young woman stood trembling outside the door of her dying mother's hospital room. Memories of the ugly words she had spoken raced through her mind. She could not erase the pain she had caused her mother by ignoring her and even laughing at her in front of others. For the first time, she understood how her mother had suffered for her sake.

As the young woman walked into the room, her mother appeared as pale as the sheets on which she lay. The grieving girl threw herself across her mother. She cried, "Mother, I'm so sorry! Can you ever forgive me? I never knew how much you suffered for me. I'm so ashamed!"

Freely she kissed her mother's face. For twenty years, the mother had waited patiently for her daughter's love. With a faint smile of joy the mother whispered, "Honey, I've already forgiven you."[3]

This story packs a powerful parenting principle. Our kids can be cruel. I have listened to some of the meanest words spoken by children to their own flesh-and-blood parents. Art Linkletter hosted a classic TV show, *Kids Say the Darndest Things*. True. And they also say some of the cruelest things, like:

- "I don't like you."
- "We have nothing in common."
- "I'm ashamed to be seen with you."
- "You don't love me."
- "I don't love you."
- "I wish you'd leave me alone."
- "I don't want to live at home with you anymore."
- "I hate you!"

As parents, we are not simply thrown into the parent trap to dig deep and fend for ourselves and try in vain to muster up affection for our child. We have a supernatural reservoir of love we can tap into at all times. God's love for us and for our child is a resource from which we can continually draw.

My son's heart broke for one simple reason as he stood with his sister on the basketball court; he loves his sister whose heart was breaking. If we dare to love, we risk being hurt. Pain and love walk hand in hand. As C. S. Lewis put it, "Love anything and your heart will be weary and possibly broken. If you want to make sure of keeping it intact you must give it to no one, not even an animal."[4]

Here is a summary of the characteristics of I-love-you-anyway families:

I-love-you-anyway families protect each other's dignity and self-worth, especially when one of their number is vulnerable and exposed.

I-love-you-anyway families are sensitive and compassionate with each other.

Parents look for opportunities to express "I love you anyway" to their children.

They use discipline for redemption not punishment.

While holding to moral absolutes, parents are able to demonstrate flexibility in their discipline.

Sometimes parents must invoke the absolute no or absolute yes.

Any parent who dares to discipline his or her son or daughter, particularly through the teenage years, will pay a price. Dr. James Dobson affirms this in the title of one of his books: *Parenting Isn't for Cowards.* At some point every parent faces logical questions: Is it worth it? Is it worth fighting over moral boundary lines? Is it worth the emotional and psychological stress to invoke the absolute yes or the absolute no?

The next chapter will help us answer these honest questions.

A Window into My Child's Heart: Protection

When I saw my mother pass me in the hallway at school, my heart sank, my face turned white as a sheet, and my mouth got as dry as the desert. I knew immediately why she was there. She wanted to talk with my English teacher about the grade I had received on my report card—an F. Since my grade was just one point from passing, my mom was certain that with a little parental encouragement my teacher would bump it up. I, however, knew that my grade was not the result of a simple mathematical calculation and that my teacher would not be inclined to give me even a one-point gift. I had not told my mother the reason for my grade.

At the beginning of the semester, the teacher tested us on our summer reading. I had not read the book, so, in a moment of desperation, I copied a classmate's answers verbatim. The following day, before passing out the graded tests, the teacher explained that three different tests had been administered. Because of this, she knew that some students had cheated. Very tricky!

Mean, but tricky. The test paper I had copied was totally different from the test I had passed in.

The teacher explained that she wouldn't tell our parents about our cheating if we confessed it to her. I stepped forward, pleaded guilty, and promptly received a zero on the test.

The day that my mom met with my English teacher, she was trying to protect me, having no idea what I had done. When she became aware of my dishonesty, she was devastated. At that moment I felt so unworthy of her love and protection, and I began to do some serious soul-searching that resulted in some changes in my life.

Fred IV

7

I Protect You

If you are a mother or a father, your most important job is to love your child with all your heart and with all your soul. . . . we all rededicate ourselves to the parenting, if we are fortunate enough to have a child.

George W. Bush

Rules without relationship lead to rebellion.

Josh McDowell

Rachel Levy was your typical seventeen year old. She grew up in Southern California's Silicone Valley. She loved to work out, sip Diet Pepsi, and listen to Pink Floyd and Christina Aguilera. She wore Tommy Girl perfume, Clinique makeup, and Victoria's Secret fruit-scented body lotion. Her favorite movies were *Pretty Woman* and *Titanic*. She filled her diary with poems about life and love, while struggling with common teenage issues—the gap between her teeth, her weight, her friends.

Following her parents' divorce, she moved to Israel with her mom and three brothers where they lived in a small apartment in Jerusalem. On Thursday night, March 28, 2002, she hung out late at the Jerusalem mall, returning home in the wee hours of the morning. The next day she woke up late, leisurely drank a cup of coffee with her mom, and then volunteered to run to the market to pick up some parsley, red pepper, and coriander for their Passover meal later that evening.

Nineteen-year-old Ayat Al-Akhras grew up less than four miles away. The two girls had never met, but under other circumstances they could have been classmates, even best friends. They were both attractive, vibrant, and highly intelligent. When their faces appeared side by side on the cover of *Newsweek,* their long black hair and deep dark eyes gave them such a striking resemblance to one another, you might have thought they were sisters.

As Rachel walked through the supermarket exit doors with her parsley and spices, Ayat was walking in. We don't know if they locked eyes or even noticed each other. All we know is that the security guard was suspicious of Ayat's loose, oversized shirt and cried out, "Wait!" In a split second at 1:49 P.M. Ayat pulled a rip cord, detonating the explosive vest she was wearing, killing herself and Rachel outside Bethlehem, Israel, on Good Friday 2002.

Every news service around the world jumped all over the story of the senseless death of these two young women. The entire world was shocked and groped for answers. Whatever happened to teenage innocence? How do you find answers for such a cold-blooded act of violence? Perceptively, President George W. Bush lamented, "When an eighteen-year-old Palestinian girl is induced to blow herself up and in the process kills a seventeen-year-old Israeli girl, the future itself is dying."

Behind the cover story of Rachel and Ayat's tragic deaths is the rest of the story—a story of the death of innocence. Ayat's parents had lived in the well-known tent camp on the Gaza Strip from which they had fled to an Arab village near Tel Aviv after the 1948 war. Her dad became supervisor of an Israeli construction firm and had above average resources enabling him to build a three-story concrete house for his eleven children. But Ayat was exposed to more than her share of hatred, violence, gunfire, bombs, and abuse. Her own brother was shot and wounded by Israeli troops. A close family friend had been shot to death while planting a roadside bomb near a Jewish settlement. On March 8 Ayat was deeply affected when Israeli guns fired in the street outside her home. To her horror, troops had shot and killed a Palestinian neighbor who was sitting in his apartment playing Legos with his daughter. Watching her brother carry the man's corpse down the stairwell was more than Ayat could stomach. Her sensitive spirit was now threadbare, mutilated. Her sensitivities were violated and she felt she could take no more.

The next week she secretly made contact with a radical Palestinian group, was trained in bombing, signed a covenant of agreement, and filmed a political statement, later released on a national news network. On that ill-fated Friday, at 7:30 A.M., she gathered her books as if leaving for class. "Please wish me well on my test today," her mother remembered her saying. According to her parents, she was the brightest of all their children. Her keen mind and sensitive spirit drew her to give up dolls for political activism at a young age. Her parting words were, "I won't see you anymore." Her parents thought that was odd. She walked through fields, skirted military checkpoints, and passed undetected into Jerusalem. Somewhere en route she met her terrorist accomplices, received her explosive vest, and found her way into the supermarket. The rest is history.

When the smoke cleared and the rubble was removed, they found two teenagers who had lost their lives to violence. One of them had already lost her innocence.[1]

As we read this emotional account, it is all too easy for us to distance ourselves. We want to think, *Aw, that is a whole world away. Crazy things happen in the Middle East. As a parent in middle-class America, I can't relate.* Not so fast. Don't kid yourself. Our culture is recklessly slaughtering innocence. Hollywood is selling it wholesale to the highest bidder at bargain basement prices. High schools treat it carelessly, crumpling it up like a useless cellophane wrapper around a CD case and tossing it in the dumpster. And our Washington, D.C., legislators don't know what to do to reverse the tragedy of this downward spiral. No, Middle East terrorism is not the only bully on the playground of our generation. What about the shootings in white, suburban Columbine High School? Or the Oklahoma City truck bomb? What about the statistics that tell us one of five women will be date raped before she graduates from college or the mutilation of the dignity of countless middle school students who feel the sting of being called "fat," "pig," "beast," "queer," or "runt"? What about the cumulative effect of the shock-violent movies and videos drenched with murder, mutilation, premarital sex, and masochism? The average high school graduate has already witnessed eighteen thousand murders on TV. That is a lot of innocence busting. We have been silently standing on the sidewalk as our culture has slaughtered innocence in the streets. It is now fair to classify innocence as an endangered species, but who will be her protector?

Innocence Redefined

When I was an adolescent, my mother told me never to date a girl who couldn't blush. She explained that if a girl had lost the innate ability to be embarrassed under certain circumstances, she had probably lost her innocence. Webster defines *innocence* as "the state of being free from sin, evil or guilt; freedom from guile, curiosity or foolishness; the inability to corrupt or injure; to do nothing morally wrong; guiltless."

The Bible exhorts us to "be wise about what is good, and innocent about what is evil" (Rom. 16:19). Or as the Phillips translation says, "I want to see you experts in good, and not even beginners in evil." Even Jesus urged his followers to be "innocent as doves" (Matt. 10:16). The Greek word translated "innocent" is *akeraious*, which means "unravaged, unharmed, that which is still in its original state, . . . intact, total moral innocence"[2] or "freedom from alien disturbing elements; integrity of the moral nature—the best sincerity; seductive teaching is instinctively repelled."[3]

Innocence is a built-in moral immunity system. It is intended to enable us—and our child—to filter out the harmful from the healthy, to discern truth from error, to distinguish between the sacred and the common, and to ward off potentially disturbing diseases. We parents know our children will face morally and ethically compromising situations and we want them to be able to navigate past the temptations and make smart choices. One of the life-giving ways I can express "I love you" to my child is by being a guardian of his innocence. This is a call too many parents have abdicated for a variety of reasons, but one that must be reclaimed. Too much of my child's potential is riding on this single issue for me to err by default.

We install antivirus software on our computers to protect them from an insidious attack on our hard drive. Shouldn't we be even more proactive as we protect our child's moral hard drive from the viruses that will attack her conscience? Our child may lose her innocence somewhere in adolescence or young adulthood, and all too frequently it is through her own choice and outside of our control. But we parents must do everything within our power to protect our children from losing their innocence through the unexpected invasion of alien intruders with evil intent.

What parent doesn't want his or her son to be unravaged, unharmed, and in his original state of intact, moral innocence? Who doesn't want his or her daughter to be free from alien or disturbing elements? What parent wouldn't want his or her child to instinctively repel seductive teaching? To ensure the life we want for our children, parental discipline becomes essential. If your child's innocence is of value to you, you will be willing to pay the price of protecting it, regardless of how much relational currency it may cost you. You will give your child the gift of carefully crafted boundary lines. You will honor him with the gift of negotiation. You will allow him the privilege of facing the consequences of his mistakes even when it costs you more than it costs your child. You will, therefore, treat your child to the gift of reality and ultimately the gift of dignity.

The Bible says of Father God, "The Lord disciplines those he loves, and he punishes everyone he accepts as a son" (Heb. 12:6). There is no punitive motive behind God's variety of loving discipline. It is devoid of anger, harshness, retaliation, pride, abuse, and insensitivity. It is full of mercy, love, kindness, concern, blessing, and benefit. Notice the connection between affection—"those He loves"—and acceptance—"everyone he accepts as a son." Affection and acceptance are wired together in discipline in a way that exceeds any other aspect of parenting. Discipline says, "I love you enough to do what I can to protect your innocence; I love you enough to hold the line, even when you temporarily hate me for it."

Innocence Rediscovered

You might be thinking, *Okay, so innocence is a virtue worth fighting for. But where do I begin?* It is easy to feel intimidated by the seemingly insurmountable odds we are up against. *How could I possibly take on our culture? And even if I could, I don't want to run the risk of isolating my child in an unhealthy way or ostracizing her from her peers, do I?*

For centuries Jewish parents have taken seriously their role in protecting innocence in the lives of their children. While it extracted a high price, they were willing to do whatever it took to protect this virtue in their sons and daughters. Following a winning plan that functioned on three strategic levels, they have exerted far-reaching influence on their sons and daughters. You may or may not be a faith person; in either case, these insights could prove helpful to you.

Level One: Parents practice personal ethics and morality in their own lives first. The lifestyle of Mom and Dad sets the tempo for the family values children will imitate and emulate. "These commandments that I give you today are to be upon your hearts" (Deut. 6:6).

Level Two: Parents teach values to their children through the casual serendipitous moments of everyday life. "Impress them on your children. Talk about them when you sit at home and when you walk along the road, when you lie down and when you get up" (v. 7).

Level Three: Parents communicate values to their children through the more formal, intentional, premeditated, structured teaching moments as well. "Tie them as symbols on your hands and bind them on your foreheads. Write them on the doorframes of your houses and on your gates" (vv. 8–9).

This threefold mentoring method doesn't necessarily guarantee success, but it certainly increases parental effectiveness.

The next logical question is, "What are the values worth modeling, mentoring, and teaching to the next generation?" The Jews had a ready answer. There were ten values by which they lived and died. These values were regarded as innocence boosters; violations of them were seen as innocence busters.

And what are these ten innocence-boosting values?

1. The Value of Recognizing One True God

As we learn to cultivate honor for God in our daily life, we set up the ultimate firewall protection against potential innocence busters. Regardless of religious preference, families that express gratitude to God for his goodness and kindness do better at expressing gratitude to each other. And families that cultivate a God-consciousness are more successful at protecting innocence because they have a higher point of reference. After all, God is the ultimate source of innocence and he is its primary protector. "You shall have no other gods before me" (Deut. 5:7).

2. The Value of Protecting Our Supreme Love for God

As we teach our children to treasure what is unseen more than what can be seen, we guard their hearts against the downward gravitational pull of hedonism, materialism, and even egotism. Fast cars, new clothes, big homes, and expensive toys are fun, but they can also be highly distracting. Material things are beneath us, while immaterial things—such as virtue, honor, dignity, conscience, purity, innocence, holiness, and certainly God himself—are above us. "You shall not make for yourself an idol in the form of anything in heaven above or on the earth beneath or in the waters below. You shall not bow down to them or worship them; for I, the LORD your God, am a jealous God, punishing the children for the sin of the fathers to the third and fourth generation of those who hate me, but showing love to a thousand generations of those who love me and keep my commandments" (Deut. 5:8–10).

3. The Value of Preserving the Honor of God's Name

Since there is nothing of greater value than God, we never want to use God's name carelessly. We would not want to hear our mother's name used recklessly or shamefully, so why tolerate the demeaning use of God's name? If anything in the universe should be kept blameless, it is God's name. In fact keeping God's name innocent will greatly increase our ability to protect innocence itself. "You shall not misuse the name of the LORD your God, for the LORD will not hold anyone guiltless who misuses his name" (Deut. 5:11).

4. The Value of Preserving the Honor of God's Day

As we teach our children to center their lives in a cause bigger than themselves, we need to encourage them to pause occasionally, reflect, and give thanks to God. This will enable them to enjoy the twin gifts of rest and peace, what the Jews call Shabbat and Shalom. After all, God is the source of every good thing we enjoy. He wants us to know that work is healthy and true rest is therefore necessary. "Observe the Sabbath day by keeping it holy, as the LORD your God has commanded you. Six days you shall labor and do all your work, but the seventh day is a Sabbath to the LORD your God. On it you shall not do any work, neither you, nor your son or daughter, nor your manservant or maidservant, nor your ox, your donkey or any of your animals, nor the alien within your gates, so that your manservant and maidservant may rest, as you do. Remember that you were slaves in Egypt and that the LORD your God brought you out of there with a mighty hand and an outstretched arm. Therefore the LORD your God has commanded you to observe the Sabbath day" (Deut. 5:12–15).

5. The Value of Honoring Our Parents

Parents set the tempo for mutual sensitivity, honor, and blessing between family members as we live honorably and teach our children to show appropriate respect. Following September 11, 2001, and the heroic action of Todd Beamer and the others who stormed the cockpit and refused to allow their plane to fly into a national landmark in Washington D.C., many research studies have been released identifying the qualities of such noble people. Most heroes have one thing in common. They were raised in a home where parents demonstrated kindness, protected innocence, cultivated sensitivity, and taught their children to respect one another. "Honor your father and your mother, as the LORD your God has commanded you, so that you may live long and that it may go well with you in the land the LORD your God is giving you" (Deut. 5:16).

6. The Value of All Life

As we teach by example the honor and dignity of all people, we instill in our child compassion, sensitivity, and kindness.

By giving resources to the poor, protecting the rights of the unborn, visiting prisoners in correctional institutions, and caring for our aging parents, we clearly communicate to our children the value of every individual, regardless of his or her lot in life. "You shall not murder" (Deut. 5:17).

7. The Value and Sanctity of Human Sexuality

I want to raise my daughter to be a one-man woman and to raise my son to be a one-woman man. It is a good idea for every parent to promote zero tolerance for pornography. Dr. James Dobson of Focus on the Family has found this issue to be the Achilles' heel in his efforts to encourage family purity in the twenty-first century. At this point it would serve the best interest of every parent to heed the principle that what we tolerate in moderation, our children will push to excess. This principle is true in reference to alcohol consumption, drug use, and sexual activity. "You shall not commit adultery" (Deut. 5:18).

8. The Value of Private Property

As we teach gratitude for what we have, respect for what belongs to others, and the wisdom to distinguish the boundary line between the two, we protect our child from countless pains. Shoplifting is a modern-day epidemic, and jealousy steals fulfillment. Being discontent with what we have is a huge thief in disguise, generating envy and covetousness, which have led too many teenagers to lie, cheat, and steal. "You shall not steal" (Deut. 5:19).

9. The Value of an Honest Answer

As we judiciously guard family trust by cultivating vulnerability, transparency, sensitivity, and honesty, we build a strong fabric of safety that will enhance our child's security. We can't afford to tolerate dishonesty, deception, or white lies under any circumstances.

A few years ago on my son's thirteenth birthday, I faced an integrity test. We were treating dear ol' mom to a pricey, twenty-dollars-a-head Mother's Day buffet after church. The age limit for the attractive half-price kid's meal was twelve. When the hostess asked me my children's ages, my birthday son looked at me as if to say, *This will be interesting; how will dad answer this one?* In an instant, I thought, *Ten bucks or my integrity?* I looked the hostess in the eye, smiled, and replied, "He is celebrating his thirteenth birthday today." Andrew looked back at me with a look of pride as if to say, *Way to go, Dad! Thanks for not selling your integrity.* I must admit, I was disappointed in myself. While I passed the test, it should not have been a struggle. A moment later I loved it when the hostess winked at me and said, "I don't think he'll eat much; since today is his birthday, we'll only charge half price." Ca-ching! "You shall not give false testimony against your neighbor" (Deut. 5:20).

10. The Value of Gratitude

As we teach our child to live with a grateful heart for what they have and a contentment to live without what they don't have, we guard them from the dry rot of covetousness. If you were to look under our Christmas tree, you might find this difficult to believe, but my wife and I never buy our children everything they requested. While we buy them plenty, we always find value in helping them realize that true fulfillment is *not* found in getting what you want as much as in appreciating what you have. "You shall not covet your neighbor's wife. You shall not set your desire on your neighbor's house or land, his manservant or maidservant, his ox or donkey, or anything that belongs to your neighbor" (Deut. 5:21).

Ten Values

By now you have probably discovered that these ten values are commonly referred to as the Ten Commandments. The Ten Commandments are more than the title of an old Charlton Heston film; they are life-giving values that will benefit every family. They are the best innocence boosters in all of history.

As a child, I was taught that if the bottle was labeled poison, with the skull and crossbones, I did not need to try it to find out. The warning label was enough for me. In the same way, there are certain warning labels we want to put on life experiences so that our children will not experiment needlessly. When parents uphold the ten values, they guard the family against daily poisons. The warning labels are in our hands. It's up to us to adequately apply them.

I love the AFLAC supplemental insurance television ads with that comical white duck who is always in the right place at the right time to quack out the correct answer: *"AFLAC!"* Each ad catches people in animated discussion regarding their need for supplemental insurance, but they can't remember the name of the company that offers the insurance. Then, out of nowhere, the duck appears and quacks, *"AFLAC!"*

Wouldn't it be great if we could purchase supplemental insurance as parents to protect our child's innocence from cultural ills when we are not around? Unfortunately, there is no company that offers such a product. That is the unique role of the home. It is our responsibility to do what we can to protect our son or daughter from the moral enemies he or she will face through the developmental years. These ten values provide ten practical ways we can proactively provide innocence protection for our child.

Rachel and Ayat are gone, but their memory still warns us about the value of innocence, particularly the innocence of our child. Innocence protection has everything to do with I-love-you parenting.

Here are some questions to consider as you think about protecting the innocence of your child:

In your home is innocence still intact? To what extent has it been damaged?

What about in your life as a parent? Are you a person of integrity? Are there ethical and moral boundary lines you refuse to compromise?

How much of your own past failure are you willing to share with your child?

Are you winning the fight for innocence?

How do you want to respond to high-impact moments, such as when your child comes clean and admits to bad conduct and possibly to a cover-up?

PART 3

Meeting Their Need for Affirmation

I Am So Pleased with You

Affirmation can come in the form of a thumbs-up from your boss, a smile of admiration from your spouse, a high five from a teammate, applause for a job well done, perhaps even a standing ovation!

Acceptance and affection express unconditional honor to our child simply because of who they are; affirmation, however, expresses honor for what they do. It is here where parenting moves into new territory. We never want to lose sight of the fact that *being* precedes *doing*. But once this solid foundation is laid, we want to tap the power of a sincere compliment for a job well done. Communicating such pleasure is like high-octane gasoline in the carburetor of our child's soul.

Father God looked his Son square in the eyes and gave him a heartfelt pat on the back when he told Jesus unequivocally, "I am so pleased with you." God announced loudly enough for others to hear, "That's my Boy!" Having assured Jesus of his acceptance—"You are my Son"—and his affection—"I love you"—he wants to express his wholehearted affirmation for his way of life. The Father was well aware of all the opposition and disapproval his Son would face. He knew about the harsh words that would sting his Son's soul, and he knew about the seductive flattery that could entice him to compromise his convictions and potentially veer him off course. At the same time Father God knew the power and influence of well-timed affirmation—"I am so pleased with you."

Affirmation spotlights our child's skills, talents, performance, and accomplishments. As we will discover in these next three chapters, our affirmation will, to some extent, affect our child's success. More than that, it will greatly influence how successful he feels. Our child is probably more starved for sincere expressions of affirmation than we will ever realize.

A Window into My Child's Heart:
Pride

Last year I was running with my school in the regional track meet. This was an important meet as we were trying to make it to the state tournament. Personally, I wanted to shave off two seconds of my best effort in the 4 x 400 meter relay.

In the event, when I was handed the baton, this guy flew past me, but I was not about to let him go. I pushed my body to the limit, but my heart was bigger than my leg muscle strength. It seemed I fainted. Before I knew what happened, I had fallen facedown on the track.

I was only ten meters from the finish line, but I had lost the baton. I came to quickly and got up, but by the time I had handed off the baton, it was too late. My team ended up finishing in fourth place.

I put my face on the ground and started to cry. I felt miserable—I had given all I had, but I caused my team to lose. As I lay there in agony, I felt someone's hand on my back and heard him crying. It was my dad. As I got up, he gave me a great big hug. We embraced and cried together. He kept calling me his cruiser and his prince. I wondered how he could call me his prince after my dismal performance. He said that he had never seen me run so hard and called me a champ.

I went to bed that night worried about what my friends would say at school the next day. Most of them had seen me take the tumble, and surely the ones who hadn't would hear about it. To my surprise the next morning I had a note on my mirror. It was a quote from Teddy Roosevelt that talked about standing strong in the midst of difficulties. My dad had stayed up the night before to find a quote that would encourage me. This meant the world to me!

Stephen

8

I Am Proud of You

This is no time for ease or comfort. It is time to dare and endure.

Winston Churchill

All men die; few men ever really live.

Braveheart

The tragedy of life is what dies inside a man while he lives.

Albert Schweitzer

Mom and Dad, never underestimate the power of a sincere and appropriate compliment. You can shape your sentence a thousand different ways, but your son or daughter is dying to hear you say, "I am so pleased with you."

When Curt Schilling of the Arizona Diamondbacks stepped to the mound in game seven of the 2001 World Series to face his mentor and opposing pitcher Roger Clemens, of the New York Yankees, it was the fulfillment of a childhood dream and then some. The stadium was packed. The air was supercharged. The attention of every sports fan in America was riveted on the opening pitch. It was a moment little boys dream of. "If the Lord had sat me down in January of this year and asked me to script out a dream season, I couldn't have come up with this," Schilling said. "Game 7 against Roger Clemens. Unbelievable! Everybody who's ever played this sport at any level has had a Wiffle ball in their hand at some point and said, 'It's the seventh game of the World Series and you're either pitching or hitting.' How cool is that?"[1]

With the Diamondbacks in the field, the umpire screamed, "Play ball!" Schilling slapped the hardball deep in the glove, took off his hat, wiped his forehead, and looked over to his wife seated on the third base line. Right next to her was an empty seat, undoubtedly the only empty seat in the stadium. It was reserved for Curt's dad, Cliff Schilling, who died in January 1988, right before Curt's first season in the majors with Baltimore. Over those years Curt has been the starting pitcher in 290 games, and there has been an empty seat reserved for his father at every one of his games. "He's never far away when I'm in a situation like this. He'd be laughing that this is happening to me and has to be pretty fired up."

Being pretty fired up is what this chapter is all about. It's about a soft spot inside every child and every big kid—like Curt Schilling—who longs to hear Dad say, "I'm so proud of you," or to hear Mom say, "I am so pleased." The fact is there may never have been a baseball, football, basketball, or any game ever played in which every competitor didn't glance into the stands to look for where Mom and Dad were seated. There has perhaps never been an awards ceremony, school play, or major public event in which every participant didn't account for his or her parents' presence or lack thereof.

What does this tell us? The point is simple yet profound. No matter how much distance comes between our child and us, somewhere down deep in his belly, he will always long for our affirmation. Despite superficial or circumstantial evidence to the contrary, every child longs to bring pleasure to his parents.

Even the hard-hearted tough guys will crack wide open when they feel their parents' pleasure. Pete Rose had a reputation for being a ruthless competitor. He mowed down more catchers in an effort to score game-winning runs than perhaps anyone in history. The night he broke the Major League Baseball record for the most lifetime hits, he broke down and sobbed like a baby. The fans went ballistic as Rose hit the ball into the outfield and rounded first base, but this tough-as-nails baseball icon proceeded to melt into a heap of emotional mush.

"Why?" interviewers asked after the game. Rose explained that the moment he realized he had broken the record, there was one image that flashed in front of his eyes. He envisioned his deceased father looking on from the heavenly bleachers. Rose rounded first base, then lifted his head, looked up into the night sky, and lost it. Pete explained that until that moment he had never felt his dad's love and affirmation. In a sense, in that instant, for the very first time in his life, he heard his dad say, "Son, I'm proud of you. Pete, I am so pleased."

An absentee parent continues to have an enormous effect on his or her child, but it is not always as positive as the impact that Schilling and Rose experienced. Some absentee parents leave deep hurts, insecurity, and confusion in their wake. Erma Bombeck was normally a funny lady. Like a modern-day prophet, she insightfully struck chords with which we can easily identify. But when she talked about her absentee dad, you could feel her pain.

> One morning my father didn't get up and go to work. He went to the hospital and died the next day. I hadn't thought that much about him before. He was just someone who left and came home and seemed glad to see everyone. He opened the jar of pickles when no one else could. He was the only one in the house who wasn't afraid to go into the basement by himself. Whenever I played house, the mother doll had a lot to do. I never knew what to do with the daddy doll, so I had him say, "I'm going off to work now"; and I put him under the bed. The funeral was in our living room, and a lot of people came and brought all kinds of good food and cakes. We never had so much company before. I went to my room and felt under the bed for the daddy doll, and when I found him I dusted him off and put him on my bed. He never did anything. I didn't know his leaving would hurt so much.[2]

I wonder how many other boys and girls have felt the same gaping hole down deep in their soul. When a mom or dad actually dies, it may be easier to handle. But when a parent is still very much alive and yet by choice or default neglects his or her child, a wound is inflicted that does not easily heal.

Special Words

For both Rose and Schilling, the screaming fans, the media hype, the interviewers, the autographs, the record books—even the fat salary checks—all paled in comparison to the affirmation of their parent. The difference for you and me as parents is that we are still alive; the similarity is that our child longs with all the passion of his or her soul to receive the nod of our delight, the smile of our pleasure in him or her. Just shake your head one time in amazement at her achievement. Just give her a thumbs-up of approval. Somehow communicate the utter joy and fulfillment she brings to you and you will stand amazed at the influence that simple gesture will have in motivating her to even greater achievement. You play a unique and strategic role in the life of your son or daughter. When Father God said to his Son, "I am so pleased with you," he spoke the words every daughter and son longs to hear. Deep down all children want to feel a sense of accomplishment. They want to know they can contribute, and they want to know that you notice.

With Father God's affirming remarks, he poured gas in the carburetor of his Son's soul. His words of acceptance—"You are my Son"—honored his Son's worth and dignity simply for who he was. As we have said, the value of *being* precedes the value of *doing*. We are all on a torturous treadmill if we think we need to gain approval through performance. If our self-worth is tied to our accomplishments, we will always feel unfulfilled to some extent, and we will live in fear of our next failure. Father God freed his Son from such bondage when he affirmed his worth based on *being*, not *doing*. When he said, "I love you," he was saying, "I enjoy just being with you. It doesn't depend on your accomplishing anything." Only after the solid foundation of dignity is laid does the Father speak to his Son's abilities: "I am so pleased with you."

While affirmation is distinct from acceptance and affection, the three are certainly related. Like family members, these three have a life of their own and yet they are healthier in relationship to each other. They feed off and encourage each other.

I—This is your God talking. I know how much my thoughts and affirmation mean to you, so I want to be clear and explicit in my expression.

Am—I enjoy watching you. You are right this minute bringing me such pleasure that I can't contain it. I just had to let you know about the way I feel toward you right now.

So—This is the word I use to add a little extra, the word of declaration, explanation, emphasis, and more. I am more than plain pleased; I am so very pleased. Watching you makes me smile as I shake my head in wonder. You are amazing, wonderful, breathtaking.

Pleased—I delight in you. I revel in you. The geographical distance between us is inconsequential. Between you and me are only pleasure, joy, goodness, and fondness. Whenever my thoughts turn to you, which happens far more than you would ever imagine, I am proud. Your life makes mine worthwhile. I celebrate you! You are everything I ever wanted in a son and more.

With you—You, Jesus, are my Son, my friend, my beloved, my joy, my crown. You're not one in a million; you are my one and only. There is no one else for whom I harbor such fondness and pleasure. I want you to feel it. I want my words to come like anointing oil that flows down over your head and your body. Your thoughts, words, attitudes, and actions are all pleasing in my sight. You make me want to stand up and dance.

After one swig from that bottle of affirmation, anything else would taste like dishwater. Why settle for soapsuds when you can drink crystal clear water? Jesus, the Son, drank in the words like spiritual Gatorade. These words brought confidence, confirmation, courage, fortitude, vision, focus, fullness, and healthy ambition. The Father's pleasure became the largest gauge on the instrument panel of Jesus' inner life. Like a compass needle, the Father's affirmation was due north, and Jesus would frequently get his bearings accordingly. Often Jesus referred to his conscious effort to please his Dad and his constant awareness of his Father's pleasure.

- I can do nothing by myself; I do only what I see the Father doing (John 5:19).
- The Father has placed his seal of approval on me (6:27).
- I only speak the words my Father gives me (8:28).
- I always do what pleases my Father (v. 29).
- My Father loves me (10:17).
- I do what my Father does (v. 37).
- I know that my Father always hears me when I pray (11:41–42).

Much like Curt Schilling, Jesus went through life looking for his Dad's smile. Every day was like a big game, only for Jesus the stakes were higher.

There is another statement that Father God made to Son God: "This is my Son, whom I love; with him I am well pleased. Listen to him!" (Matt. 17:5). These words are virtually identical to the statement at his baptism, except in this case, the words are in the third person. Rather than being spoken to the Son, they are spoken to the followers of the Son about the Son. Additionally, the exhortation, "Listen to him," is included. These added words further reinforce the affirmation, essentially saying, "He is a good talker; it's worth paying close attention to what he has to say." While these words were not spoken to Jesus, you can be sure they were a delight to his ears. The only thing better than personally receiving a sincere compliment is publicly receiving a sincere compliment—when others hear of your honor, worthiness, and success.

Applause

We sometimes forget that seated near us in the bleachers of our child's life are a host of other fans and even a few critics. Pleasing the fans and appeasing the critics may be stronger motivations in the life of our child than we care to admit. To call it a fan club is probably an overstatement, but every child, in one form or another, has his own personal gallery—a group of people who know him, walk with him, and critique his performance. They continually render either approval or disapproval. Knowing the various personalities in your child's gallery can be a great asset to your parenting influence.

Friends: It may drive us crazy when our third-grade son wants to wear his denim cargo pants to school every day. If we do our research, we may discover that sixth-grader Derek, who sits next to him on the school bus, told him they were cool.

Boyfriend or girlfriend: When your seventh-grade daughter insists on getting her leg tattooed, you may discover that her eighth-grade heartthrob, Jared, already has a tattoo on his leg.

Teachers and coaches: When we find it curious—even baffling—that our son suddenly wants to teach political science as a future career, it may well be linked to the influence of his current poli-sci teacher.

Ministers and religious leaders: If our daughter suddenly gets religious and wants to be at church every time the doors are opened, it may well be traced to an effective spiritual mentor.

Authors, actors, songwriters, rock stars, sports heroes, opinion makers: Role models come in various shapes and sizes. Parents might as well accept the fact that they cannot select their child's star.

God: As odd as it may sound, many children are legitimately sensitive to the Spirit of God. Our son or daughter may be spiritually tuned in to God's applause. He or she may be highly motivated to please God. Yes, the invisible presence of God himself may have a place in your child's bleachers.

These various voices need not intimidate or infuriate us. Instead, they should motivate us to keep our voice in the arena. As we have said, a parent's primary role is to be a mirror or sounding board to help his or her child accurately define reality. All things being equal, we parents know our children better than anyone else. We, of all people, should have a primary voice as they shape their self-image and make life choices related to college, career, life partner, value system, and faith.

We dare not abdicate our role as chief cheerleader. Our stock may be temporarily down on our child's exchange; we may feel like we lack parental currency; we may be the dubious recipient of a get-lost attitude, but we can rest assured that no one is better equipped and better qualified to give our son or daughter an accurate view on reality than we are. The primary role of identity shaping and affirmation belongs to us. No one in our child's life can do it as well as we can. This is a parenting principle to remember: Parent with affirmation and praise. Be sure your voice is consistently heard in your child's arena. Applause is a powerful magnet we parents want to use liberally.

Praise God

What could be more powerful than praising your child? For those of us who are people of faith, there is something more powerful and perhaps more appropriate—praising God for your child, in front of your child. Praising God for the gifts, talents, qualities, and passions that God has given him is legitimate and something your child should often hear.

Oni Kittle is a good friend and a great parent. At a time in her son's life when he was gaining great success and wealth in the business community, his spiritual pursuits were less notable. As a Christian mom who was certainly grateful for God's goodness to her son yet burdened over his lack of recognition of God as the source of his success, Oni wisely noticed a life-giving parenting principle in the Bible. Referring to people like her son, she read, "For although they knew God, they neither glorified him as God nor gave thanks to him, but their thinking became futile and their foolish hearts were darkened" (Rom. 1:21).

As she read these words, a light went on. God was indeed blessing her son, and she wanted to appropriately rejoice with him in his success. At the same time, she wanted to point her son to God, the ultimate source of his prosperity and achievement, but she wanted to avoid sounding pious or awkwardly religious. Suddenly she realized that until he would give thanks to God, she could do it for him. Without preaching or pointing a goading finger, she could affirm her son's success and praise the Lord simultaneously. She would say things like, "You are so smart! God has sure blessed you with a wonderful mind. Your dad and I are so proud of you. God has blessed you beyond anything we imagined. Your success in business is a tribute to how well you are using the gifts God has given you."

After a few months of these God-centered and yet son-affirming statements, her son began to restructure his priorities. He began to pursue and develop a love relationship with God. He returned to consistent church attendance and even began tithing his substantial income to need-meeting projects through his local church.

Praising our child is powerful. Praising our God for our child is even more powerful.

Affirmation Flows from Acceptance and Affection

A parent's accurate view of his or her child's talents, gifts, and passions is vital to effective affirmation. Misguided compliments, on the other hand, can be as useless and counterproductive as Saddam Hussein's scud missiles. We want our words to be wise, well timed, and well directed. This means that initially we must accept our child for who she is.

Acceptance comes first. To reverse the sequence could result in pointing our son or daughter in the wrong direction. For example, if our child weighs 220 pounds in the sixth grade, high jump or hurdles is probably not the best pursuit for success in track and field. However, the shot put may be just the right niche. Parenting our child to aspire for a state medal could well be appropriate, but it must be in the right event.

Just as acceptance is a prerequisite to affirmation, so is affection. Children don't care how much parents know until they know how much they care. This is more than just a clever twist of words. It is a rock solid parenting principle. Affection forms the context for our relationship. Once our child feels our acceptance and our affection, he will be motivated to give weight to our words of affirmation. It is possible, though, for parents to accept their child for who he is and shower him with affection and yet cheat him out of the essential element of affirmation on which he would thrive. Within every child's heart is the longing to hear his parents say, "You make me proud." You and I have the privilege to respond to that longing.

Our child will gravitate to the loudest applause—or the applause to which she attributes the highest value. The sources of applause are multiple and we would do well to realize that our hand clap is not the only one coming from the bleachers of our child's life. In a sense we have no control over the value she places on our applause compared to the affirmation of others. There is, however, a definite connection between the level of confidence she has in our acceptance and our affection and the weight she puts on our affirmation. At the same time, we might as well accept the fact that, at different phases of childhood development, our own applause stock may go up or down like the NASDAQ, depending on a complex variety of factors.

Perhaps you have seen the following anonymously written sequence:

4 years: My Daddy can do anything!

7 years: My Dad knows a lot, a whole lot.

8 years: My father does not know quite everything.

12 years: Well, naturally, Father does not know that either.

14 years: Oh, Father? He is hopelessly old-fashioned.

21 years: Oh, that man—he is out of date!

25 years: He knows a little bit about it, but not much.

30 years: I must find out what Dad thinks about it.

35 years: Before we decide, we will get Dad's idea first.

50 years: What would Dad have thought about that?

60 years: My dad knew literally everything!

65 years: I wish I could talk it over with Dad once more.

As Mark Twain, with his typically dry humor, aptly stated, "When I was thirteen I thought my dad was the dumbest guy in the world; when I turned seventeen, I couldn't believe how much he had learned in four years." If your son or daughter is not putting much stock in your applause right now, don't sell out and don't worry. Time is on your side. Sooner or later, your stock is bound to go up.

Here are some things to think about concerning your expression of pride in your child:

Are you on your child's own personal cheerleading squad? Does he frequently hear your voice cheering his name?

Are you learning to recognize the other voices in the bleachers of your daughter's life?

Is your stock currently up or down in your child's portfolio?

A Window into My Child's Heart: Freedom

One Christmas, when I was home from college for the holidays, our family sat down for dinner and shared memories of the past year.

After dinner Dad handed to each of my brothers and me an envelope containing a handwritten letter. Little did I know what an impact my father's gift would have on my life. That Christmas my father gave me the gift of freedom—greater than any present that could have been wrapped and placed beneath a tree. It was a gift of affirmation and empowerment. It affirmed who I am and empowered me to become even greater. It implored me to dream big dreams, take risks, be my own person, live courageously and adventurously, and listen only to the voice of my heavenly Father.

My father was encouraging me to step out as an adult into the life God wants for me. His words of love and his confidence in me were gifts that every child longs to receive.

Andrea

9

I Release You

My country did not send me 5,000 miles to start the race—they sent me 5,000 miles to finish the race.

> John Stephen Akhwari,
> 1968 Olympic marathon runner from Tanzania,
> who, bloodied and bandaged, finished last

For this reason a man will leave his father and mother and be united to his wife, and the two will become one flesh.

> Genesis 2:24

We began this book with a swig from the carafe of parenting fulfillment as I told my story of being best man in my firstborn's wedding. As we approach the end of the book, we want to consider the wedding from an entirely different perspective—that of the father of the bride.

Comedian Steve Martin certainly brought new meaning to the concept of father of the bride in the movie by that title. Virtually the only wedding decision he had to make was when to write the checks to pay the bills. On every other issue, he was way down the totem pole of decision makers, somewhere between eighteenth and twentieth.

In this wedding saga, the father is almost a tragic figure. At his only moment of glory, while walking arm-in-arm next to his pride and joy down the center aisle in front of a packed house, no one even notices him—all eyes are on the bride. And at the front of the auditorium, eager to replace him at his daughter's elbow, is a mere kid, a young, inexperienced, superficial, naïve boy, getting drool stains on the lapel of his rented tuxedo as he considers his catch. The young man is in an emotional three-point stance and can't wait until his father-in-law-to-be steps aside. He has absolutely no concept of how much has been invested in this moment and is literally incapable of imagining what is inside the chest cavity of his bride's dad. No one has a clue how many sleepless nights he spent waiting up past his daughter's curfew and how much college tuition he had to pay. No one knows how many silent tears of compassion, how many hours of prayer, and how many late-night talks preceded this brief experience of walking his daughter down the aisle. And then, the father of the bride is supposed to give a one-, two-, or three-word answer to the most audacious question routinely asked in the civilized world—"Who gives this woman to be married to this man?" As a young minister, I admit I used to ask those words glibly. Not anymore. I have found the older my daughter gets, the more weighty and poignant those words become. At times it seems as though it could almost be paraphrased,

"Who in their right mind would give their daughter to be married to this man?" Nowhere else in the western world is something so valuable asked for so casually. Someday I wouldn't blame a dad if he hauled off and slugged me for asking such a question.

As comical as this scene might appear, it represents a much larger parenting principle we can all take to heart. Release is vital for effective parenting. A great deal of parenting is hands-on, but some of the most critical parenting is hands-off. Wisdom is required to know the difference between the two.

Hands-Off Parenting

Acceptance is primarily hands-on, and so is affection. Affirmation, however, moves us into the somewhat threatening, awkward, uncharted waters of hands-off parenting. It is not surprising that hands-off parenting is contrary to our instincts. In infancy, children are held, cradled, diapered, burped, fed, bathed, clothed, and changed—all hands-on. In childhood, they are hugged, instructed, guided, read to, wrestled with—largely hands-on. In adolescence, they are counseled, released, chauffeured, dropped off, cooked for, watched, cheered for, sent out—quite often hands-on.

Like eagles, children were never intended to spend their lives in the nest. Just trace the systematic progression of effective hands-off parenting.

1. The very act of conception involves release. The wife releases her egg into the uterus, and the husband releases his sperm to swim ecstatically up the vaginal corridor. The union of these forty-six chromosomes begins to

immediately operate as a life all its own—all because of the initial release.

2. Birth is another moment of parental release. Despite the intimate parental bond between mother and prenatal infant, there comes a moment of incredible discomfort when retaining the baby seems far less desirable than discharging it. Though the process is overwhelmingly painful, release is the natural option.

3. Placing the baby in his own cradle in his own room is one step in hands-off parenting.

4. Infancy provides many opportunities for release. Sherry and I were taught a handy parenting guideline: If you allow your child to cry herself to sleep when she is too young, she will be insecure; and if you don't allow her to cry herself to sleep by a certain age, she will be insecure. It made sense to us.

5. Hands-off parenting progresses as we leave the baby for the first time with a babysitter.

6. Then we leave our child at preschool or day care.

7. We teach our child to ride a bike and then let go so he can ride on his own.

8. We watch our child get on the school bus for the first time.

9. We give her permission to spend the night at a friend's house or attend her first slumber party.

10. We give our child the keys to the car and watch him drive out of the driveway.

11. We say yes to the high school boy who asks permission to date our daughter.

12. We drop our child off at college.

And the list goes on.

What do each of these release moments have in common? They each make a powerful statement of affirmation to our child. They each say, "You can do it. I have complete confidence in you to fulfill what is required of you as you step out. You will do great. You have what it takes to meet the challenges you face." That is affirmation through and through.

As a pastor, I have stood at the elbow of many hospitalized children, with a front-row seat to some of the finest "you're-going-to-make-it" parenting speeches of all time. Any ER nurse will tell you that the confidence of family members often does more to pull a child through life-threatening moments than doctors, nurses, and medical treatment can do.

Whether we are dropping our children off for their first day at kindergarten or their first day of college, watching them drive out of the driveway or walking them down the aisle, release is a vital skill of effective parenting. It is an appropriate way of saying many things:

I believe in you.

You are your own person.

You are on your own, but I am there to help if you need me.

I trust you.

You da man!

You've got skills.

You're smart.

You're capable.

You're qualified, more than qualified.

Knock 'em dead!

I have confidence in you.

You have what it takes.

You can do it.

I know you can!

Passing the Baton

In high school I ran the mile relay. I trained hard and practiced long. I learned that in addition to speed, races were won or lost in the handoff. A bobbled baton or a mistimed transition could cost the faster team the gold medal.

Effective hands-off parenting is no less important than effective hands-on parenting. If we suddenly become insecure, indecisive, tentative, or reluctant, we can all too easily bobble or even drop the baton. We dare not release the baton too soon nor hold on too long.

Parenting is a relay. Our parents passed us the baton, and, at a critical moment, it is ours to pass on to our children. The distance is more than a mile—it's a generation. The stakes are higher—not gold, silver, or bronze, but a legacy. Good parenting, like a good relay team, will practice the passing of the baton many times.

For parents who are faith people, there is no more vital issue to us than our child's relationship with God. There is a great deal of hands-on parenting invested in our child's spiritual life—bedtime prayers, family Bible reading, great Christian biographies, Sunday school, church attendance, Christian doctrine classes. The list goes on.

Despite our finest efforts, however, our child's relationship with God involves his own autonomous God-choice, independent from Mom and Dad. As the saying goes, God has no grandchildren. This means that I cannot run my child's leg of the spiritual relay for him; I can't even take the baton for him. He needs to grab the baton of faith for himself, and only he can run his race.

If a person is to come to personal faith in the living God, God must reveal himself to the person, and he or she must respond to God's revelation. What this means is quite profound. Despite our finest efforts of hands-on parenting to influence our child toward a love relationship with God, her response remains her choice, not ours. Therefore, this moment of eternal consequences and of ultimate importance is, bottom line, a hands-off parenting moment.

While praying for my four children last year, I realized one of the most sobering parenting principles. It suddenly dawned on me that if I do not give my children the option of rejecting my faith, I never truly give them the opportunity to embrace it. Take a deep breath and reread that sentence again. As unsettling as it sounds, our child needs to have permission to accept or reject our God. For the life of me, I can't think of a more humbling rejection. There is no more significant, far-reaching decision our child will ever make than to choose his God—the basis for his worldview, his value system, his purpose in life, his destiny. This becomes the ultimate test of our parenting. If we can release this choice to our child with full confidence (in God and in him), we will be able to empower our child for his other significant life choices as well.

My wife was at her mother's hospital bedside the days and moments prior to her death. They were precious moments of profound consequence. Her mom spoke with her about her values, her love, her lifetime of fulfillment, her pleasure with Sherry's husband (that's me!), her delight in each of our four children, and even her anticipation of eternity with God. They laughed. They prayed. They sang. They reminisced through a lifetime of memories. They cried. Nurses would quietly step in, knowing they were standing on holy ground. For a while time seemed to stand still. For Sherry those moments oozed acceptance, affection, and affirmation.

As I watched, I thought of all the effective hands-on parenting my mother-in-law had done. She was present for the birth of each of her thirteen grandchildren. Her hands knit sweaters and booties for each. She held, fed, burped, diapered, cradled, bathed, and rediapered each of our newborn babies. She sat on the sidelines of countless basketball, baseball, soccer, and football games, screaming, clapping, and making her affirming grandmother's presence known.

Outside the hospital room was a brilliant yellow-leafed maple tree with leaves that were waving good-bye. The crisp early November Michigan weather was signaling autumn. As I looked back and forth between the maple tree in the yard and my mother-in-law in the room, I couldn't help but see a striking similarity. Botanists tell us that autumn leaves fall not because they are dying but because the new life of next year's leaves is coming behind. In reality leaves on dead or dying trees do not fall; leaves on healthy or living trees are the ones that drop. Sherry's mom was experiencing new life pushing her into eternity. She had passed the baton well. She had fulfilled her purpose. She had communicated blessings at every level. She was ready to meet her Maker, and she was prepared for the ultimate hands-off parenting moment—the moment of death.

A few days later when the people in a jam-packed church sanctuary stood to their feet during her funeral to sing Handel's "Hallelujah Chorus," it was remarkable to look at her four children, thirteen grandchildren, and hundreds of close friends sensing the fulfillment of a heavenly affirmation: "Well done, my good and faithful servant. You have lived and parented well." She ran and finished her race. Now it was time for her to pass the baton. This is a moment we will all face. It is the ultimate test of hands-off parenting.

It is not until after we let go that we are able to receive back some of the sweetest, most enriching fulfillment we will ever experience. It is only after we release our children that they will be free to turn back to us with legitimate gratitude.

As you think about your hands-off parenting, consider these questions:

What part of hands-off parenting do you like?

What part drives you up the wall?

How have you already practiced the fine art of release?

What decisions are you already allowing your child to make?

A few years ago I wrote my dad a poem of honor for Father's Day. The next time I had opportunity to visit with him in his studio, I couldn't help but notice it hanging nicely framed on his wall.

If Not for You

It seems we're always on the run,
But thank the Lord, the time has come
For me to bring on back to you
Those precious moments thru which I grew.
I'd never known them . . . if not for you.

Like rowing boats and fishing, too
And catching crabs right next to you.
Showing the ring-neck snake I caught
All tied up in a little knot.

Like Little League games galore
With umps who couldn't keep the score;
Making malteds and Taylor ham
And putting spillways in the dam.

The mystery of the sugar trees
And grandiose bedtime stories.
Well-worn jokes to make us laugh
That nearly split our sides in half.

We'd go sprinting in the sand
And then play catch with mitt in hand.
Making snowmen look so real
Then flatly stating, "No big deal."
Always time to talk things out
Even thru those years of doubt.
A supportive smile that says you care
And open hand that's always there.

Now my kids can see in you
A strength they'll only find in few.
An example of a man of God
Who knows His staff and His rod.

Yes, dear Dad, the time has come
For me to say to you, "Well done."
And as I grew I always knew
That it has been because of you.

A Window into My Child's Heart: Empowerment

I currently find myself in the biggest transition of my life. Two months ago I completed graduate school. Four weeks ago, my wife and I found out that we are expecting our first child. Two weeks ago, I interviewed for a job that was an ideal fit, except for the fact that it would take us half a country away from both sets of parents. The job was offered, and we were faced with a major decision.

At this critical point, my dad sent us a timely letter. He explained that the Lord has been preparing us to be released. My wife, Jo, and I both grew up in solid homes. We were arrows being trained to hit the target. Dad explained that following the Lord's plan would not always be a cakewalk. This was so encouraging and confidence building for us.

After much prayer and soul-searching, we decided to take the job. We are confident we are headed in the right direction.

Fred IV

10

I Empower You

Now that my ladder's gone, I must lie down where all the ladders start, in the foul rag-and-bone shop of the heart.

William Butler Yeats

Whether your faith is that there is a God or that there is not a God, if you don't have any doubts you are either kidding yourself or you are asleep. Doubts are the ants in the path of faith. They keep it awake and moving.

Frederick Buechner

Empowerment has become a managerial buzzword in today's business community. It refers to the positive influence that one team member can have on another when each trusts the other enough to give permission to succeed. Empowerment is also a winning parenting principle on which our sons and daughters thrive.

Dr. Ravi Zacharias is a brilliant Christian apologist; he is also a world-class dad. With his permission, I want to share with you two powerful letters of empowerment written to his children at critical transitional moments of their development. When his firstborn, Sarah, was preparing to go off to college, he wrote her a treasured letter, excerpts of which are quoted below. Notice the heavy doses of acceptance, affection, and affirmation. Don't miss his release and empowerment.

8/21/93

> *The next few years may impart to you much knowledge, but above all may you have the wisdom to separate the worthy from the unworthy. In many ways your relationship with all of us will change, but if it is handled rightly, it will change for the better as we learn to love each other more deeply.*

> *. . . I am also certain, honey, that you will face some lonely days and nights. There will be days when you may want to pack it all up and return. One of the most difficult but precious lessons I learned at college was to endure the courses and the professors that seemed completely irrelevant or unimportant to my life's goals. Yet, in time to come I found out that the endurance I had to show during the unwanted was what prepared me best for courage and determination in the ministry. That lesson is true for all life.*

> *I want to make a few promises to you. First and foremost, that you are and will be loved more than you can ever imagine. Which means that **any time** and for **any need** please feel confident that when you call we will be there to help.*

*Secondly, that you will be prayed for daily and at
that several times. God gave you to us for all these
years and now in these most significant years ahead
we place you in his hands where you are safest.*

*Above all I have said, sweetheart, most important
to me and to you are the words of God to all of us
when he said, "Above all, guard your heart." That
will be my prayer for you, honey, that your heart will
be guarded from all people and thoughts that would
seek to turn you away.*

*. . . so let us hold fast to a positive attitude and
optimistic spirit, for that will take you through this
challenging course. Be careful and be assured that
there are four people back here whose lives are
incomplete without you.*

The second letter, perhaps even more passionate and personal, was given to his son-in-law on the night he married
Ravi's daughter. Dr. and Mrs. Zacharias had just given Sarah's
hand to him in marriage; now he is giving some words of
wisdom and a great deal of empowerment.

Dear Jeremy,

*It is virtually impossible to put into words what
goes through a father's heart when he hands his
daughter into the trust of another man. But at the
same time the comfort that comes from knowing
the man is a godly and gentle individual cannot be
gainsaid.*

*And so on this very treasured day in our lives,
we commit Sarah to you and of course have placed
her in the hands of God. I have purposely said very
little over these months by way of advice because I*

*knew you were under the counsel of the finest in Joe
Novenson. But now as the day is upon us, may I just
say two very brief words of encouragement.*

*First and foremost, Jeremy, love her with all your
heart and be kind to her at all times. A woman's heart
is very determined, but also very easily wounded.
Be to her a source of encouragement and repose. Be
your kindest when it is hardest to express tenderness.
The rewards you will gain from God will be
immeasurable because in return you will enjoy a love
that is distinctly that of a woman. God has framed us
with those needs and strengths.*

*The second thing I want to say is to be strong
in honoring your vows. The standards of the world
are constantly on a downward spiral. Keep your
standards high so that there will never be room for
temptation or dishonor. I urge you with all my heart
to take this counsel seriously. I have met too many
broken lives that took small liberties with dreadful
consequences.*

*Last, but not least, we now welcome you as our
son. We are proud of you, Jeremy. Even as I have
watched you over these months you have shown
yourself to be a gentleman and a tender, caring
individual. This is a reflection of your fine family and
we are now privileged to know the rest of them. May
God bless you, son, and give you many wonderful
years in establishing a beautiful home.*
With Love,
[Ravi Zacharias]

It is refreshing to learn that Ravi Zacharias is not only
able to defend the Christian faith as a guest lecturer at Har-

vard University, he is also able to pass on the baton of faith to his own children. Thanks, Ravi, for modeling the reality of effective parenting for the rest of us. Our friendship has enriched my life.

Visionary Leadership

Parenting without vision is like taking the family camping in a canvas tent and leaving the interior posts at home. We will survive, stay dry and protected from the elements, but it will be tough to maneuver, and we will feel as though we are suffocating. To talk about the future and paint a picture of where we are going is like setting up poles inside the tent. Every legitimate goal is like a post that lifts life's canvas off our backs and enables us to move around without encumbrance.

In the spring our front yard had to be dug up to install a new drain field for our septic tank—not once but twice! Being the tightwad I am, I encouraged (bribed) my boys to assist me with grading, raking, over-seeding, and fertilizing. The first time was tedious and painful. Twenty blisters and several weekends later, we were sore in body and in spirit. That was bad enough. The second time I thought I had mutiny on my hands! My boys wanted to jump ship. We had donned our gloves. The wheelbarrow was in place. The rakes, shovels, and buckets were ready on the outside, but on the inside we seriously lacked motivation.

How can we pull this off? I wondered. *I might get my grass planted, but I don't want to uproot my relationship with my boys in the process.* Suddenly the answer rose like the morning sun. "Hey, men, I want you to picture the thick, lush, green grass that will cover our front yard. Imagine mowing it. Ah, Stephen, pick up the rake and make a pile of all the rocks in that area over there. I want you to picture the football games we will have on the grass this fall. Andrew, you will go out for a long pass and I will throw it to you just over your left shoulder; you'll reach out and haul it in! By the way, Andrew, I want you to pick up all those large rocks and throw them in the wheelbarrow. Can you imagine the Wiffle ball games we will have out here, the croquet, the boccie ball, the badminton? I am going to whip you all in badminton this summer!" They smiled. Their eyes glinted with eager anticipation as they caught the vision.

I knew I had them with me the moment I saw their eyes light up and we started to talk about badminton instead of dirt and rocks. There we were, standing on nothing but barren, Georgia red clay, but we were trash-talking badminton. We had exchanged the mundane for a vision. We concluded our duties that afternoon in record time—faster and more efficiently than the first time, and morale was at an all-time high. Why? Because they saw the purpose. They could taste the football, Wiffle ball, croquet, and badminton. Work is always easier when every player has the end in view. So it is with parenting and family life.

Our challenge is not only to paint motivating pictures of a front lawn athletic field, but to create a vision of a mission field, a life purpose, a destiny. The words Father God spoke to his Son were clear and compelling words of vision, mission, purpose, and destiny—words of passion and zeal.

One of my children's favorite annual activities is goal setting. We call them SMART goals. SMART is an acronym, which stands for specific, measurable, achievable, realistic, and time-specific goals. Each year I sit down with each child one-on-one and offer to coach him or her in personal goal setting. The entire process, and each specific goal, is entirely the child's choice. The children are not pressured into it or made to feel awkward if they choose not to participate. They are challenged to consider goals in each area of their lives: spiritual, academic, intellectual, social, physical, recreational, financial, and moral goals. Because I guard their dignity and privacy, it is not my place to disclose their goals. I can assure you, however, that the process has always proven valuable and rewarding.

While home from college a couple years ago on Christmas vacation, Andrea said, "Dad, I love this goal setting! It gives my life direction and helps me keep my life purpose in view at all times." That comment was like a kiss on the lips.

Passionate Living

Vision quickly translates into passion. When our child catches a glimpse of a compelling vision, his heart beats faster. A gleam enters his eye, and a smile begins at the corners of his lips.

Passion has been called soul-hunger—a burning desire to achieve and fulfill a mission. Soul-hunger and soul-health go hand in hand. Healthy souls, like healthy bodies, are naturally hungry. During adolescence, I had a notoriously ravenous appetite. My mother knew that if I was not hungry, I was either sick or in love. If I refused seconds at the dinner table during high school, my dad would often inquire with a grin, "What's her name?" Similarly, if our adolescent is not hungry for her future, if she is not passionate about life, she is in some way soul-sick. While we cannot ignite passion in our child's soul, we can certainly fan the flame. This is the work of affirmation and vision casting.

Healthy people are passionate people—passionate about fulfilling their life purpose. Eric Liddell is a good example. In the classic film *Chariots of Fire*, when asked by his prodding sister about his intention to become a missionary to China, he replied, "Jenny, God made me for a purpose. He made me for China. But he also made me fast, and when I run I feel his pleasure."

Jim Elliot was a person who faced life with healthy missionary zeal. While a student at Wheaton College, he would select cafeteria food that would prepare his body for missionary service. Similarly, he excelled on the wrestling team, conditioning himself physically as well as mentally to fulfill his life purpose. He wrote, "I have determined for my life, wherever I am to be all there; whatever I do be all in it, and whatever I believe to be the will of God for my life, live it to the hilt."[1]

Live it to the hilt indeed! Following college graduation, he joined a team of buddies with a common life calling— going to Ecuador to tangibly express God's love to the little-known Auca Indian tribe. Despite evident dangers, risks, and warnings, they prayerfully pressed on, motivated by a legitimate compassion for the eternal destiny of the Aucas, the people to whom they would literally give their lives. As young pioneer missionaries, the bodies of Jim Elliot and four other members of his mission team were found dead, brutally murdered by the people they were seeking to reach. But before we cry, "What a waste!" allow me to give an epilogue to the story.

Last summer, while visiting the Christian community in Ecuador, I saw a copy of the recently translated Auca Bible, utilized by hundreds of Auca believers. In fact the Auca Indians have sent out some of their own tribespeople as missionaries to other unreached tribes, and they have in turn been martyred in the process. They were taught well by a man who wholeheartedly invested his life in what he believed to be of ultimate value. The meaning of life is found not in its duration but in its significance.

Passion looks its adversaries in the eye like Clint Eastwood and defiantly states, "Go ahead. Make my day!" Passion is the smile on the face of a challenge, a gleam in the eye of mission, a bounce in the stride of opportunity, adrenaline in the bloodstream of purpose. It says to an obstacle, "Bring it on!" It says, "Tell me I can't. Call me a name. I don't care what you throw at me. I'll prove you wrong. I'll show you what I'm made of. I can overcome. I will win."

Prior to his martyrdom, Jim Elliot expressed his passion for his life calling this way:

Am I ignitable? God deliver me from the dread asbestos of "other things." Saturate me with the oil of the Spirit that I may be aflame. But flame is transient, often short-lived. Canst thou bear this, my soul—short life? In me there dwells the Spirit of the Great Short-Lived, whose zeal for God's house consumed Him. Make me Thy fuel, flame of God.[2]

Similarly, C. S. Lewis communicated his concern over the lukewarm commitment level of many faith people: "Our Lord finds our desires not too strong but too weak. We are halfhearted creatures. We are far too easily pleased."[3] Contemporary theologian John Piper carries the same burden: "Sin is trying to quench our unquenchable soul-thirst anywhere but in God. Or more subtly, sin is pursuing satisfaction in the right direction but with lukewarm, halfhearted affections. No halfhearted, polite, dutiful religiosity here!"[4]

A century earlier Mark Twain threw down a gauntlet to his generation: "Twenty-five years from now you will be more disappointed by the things you didn't do than by the ones you did, so throw off the bowline, sail away from the safe harbor. Catch the trade winds in your sails. Explore. Dream."[5]

Passion is a fair meter by which to monitor our children. To call it a "passionometer" might be too cute for some, but if it works for you, use it. Regardless, passion for life is perhaps the most important gauge on the dashboard of our child's inner life for us to monitor. It's the single gauge that gives a combined reading when our child's tanks are filled with acceptance, affection, and affirmation.

As a young man, Jonathan Edwards, one of the greatest thinkers in U.S. history, wrote a series of resolutions that would serve as unifying principles for his adult life. One of them read: "Number Six: Resolved to live with all my might while I do live." Living with all our might is what passion is all about.

When our child's tanks of acceptance, affection, and affirmation are filled, the combined effect will be demonstrated in their zest to pursue their life purpose. It can be accurately said that acceptance brings security, affection brings stability, affirmation brings success, and combined they bring significance.

Acceptance	→	Security
Affection	→	Stability
Affirmation	→	Success
		Significance

There is good evidence that God evaluates our lives according to a form of passionometer. Speaking to a listless group of anemic followers, he said, "I know your deeds, that you are neither cold nor hot. I wish you were either one or the other! So because you are lukewarm—neither hot nor cold—I am about to spit you out of my mouth" (Rev. 3:15–16). Halfhearted devotion is not only insulting to God; it is nauseating. On the contrary, the level of wholehearted devotion he expects is well communicated in the Jews' bull's-eye text from their holy Scriptures: "Love the LORD your God with all your heart and with all your soul and with all your strength" (Deut. 6:5). And again the New Testament writers similarly appeal for passion: "Whatever you do, work at it with all your heart" (Col. 3:23).

Jesus demonstrated passionate living. It was said of him: "Zeal for your house will consume me" (John 2:17). Jesus lived with his tanks filled—his Father God made sure of that. As a result, his life, though short, was characterized by passion.

Is it any wonder that the early followers of Christ were similarly wholehearted? On numerous occasions, it was said that they devoted themselves to their ministry (see Acts 1:14; 2:42, 46; 6:4). The Greek word *proskartereo,* translated "devoted," is the strongest word for commitment used in the Greek language. It means to grab on for all you're worth and refuse to let go, to adhere tenaciously, to unrelentingly pursue. It is the Green Beret or Navy Seal level of commitment—perhaps the New York City firefighter level of commitment. Like a pit bull that sinks its teeth into a piece of raw meat and refuses to let go, like a heat-seeking missile that locks onto the heat source and refuses to veer off course until it strikes its target—that is the level of devotion Father God appropriately and effectively implanted in his one and only Son. That is also the level of devotion he implants in his healthy followers today. And that is the same level of devotion we long to see in our healthy children as they passionately pursue their own unique life purpose. We don't simply want to raise good kids who do good things; we want to raise godly kids who hit the targets for which they were destined, kids fueled by acceptance, affection, and affirmation.

Impacting the Next Generation

Before we finish, a word needs to be said about the important role grandmothers and grandfathers have in our families. Second only to Mom and Dad, they have the capacity of showering children with acceptance, affection, and affirmation. An ounce of Grandma beats a pound of generic babysitter any day.

When I was growing up, we lived close to both sets of grandparents, which greatly enriched my life. They would take me to watch baseball in Yankee Stadium, trout fishing, deep-sea fishing, and hunting. We would vacation together and weekend together. Often when I played Little League baseball, they would come and watch me pitch. Their love and support fueled my soul.

A year ago, I sat at a lunch table with my two teenage sons, my aunt and uncle, and my mom and dad, who were celebrating their sixtieth wedding anniversary. My uncle started, "Grandpa served ten terms in the U.S. Congress. He was the youngest congressman ever elected, only twenty-four years old. You can't get any younger than that! In fact by law you must be twenty-five, but he turned that magic age just days before being sworn into office." I listened intently to every detail.

My dad continued, "As a young congressman, Grandpa was assigned to the Labor Committee. It was at a time in our nation's history following the industrial revolution when labor unions were becoming so strong in protecting the blue-collar work force that something needed to be done to balance the power between labor and management. Many of the senior members of Congress, who normally would have been selected to chair the Labor Committee, declined the dubious honor— for fear of losing the next election. So they asked Grandpa if he would be willing to take it."

"He had to think through the consequence of this assignment; he knew it would cost him dearly," my uncle continued.

"Grandpa wanted to serve his country, so, despite the risk, he accepted the challenge. He was truly a devoted public servant. One of his memorable sayings was, 'The joy of living is found in a life of service,' and he lived up to it."

"In a sense it was really the luck of the draw," my dad added. "He was the youngest congressman, given one of the heaviest responsibilities."

"It did cost him dearly." My uncle's eyes moistened. His voice cracked. It was then for the first time I realized the pain that my dad and uncle had felt through my grandfather's years of public service. "He received all kinds of hate mail. He would get on the elevator with people from the labor union and the door would close, and he didn't know if he'd get off the elevator alive. It required incredible courage. It was a very fearful time for me," my uncle said. "I really had to grow up without a father. He was in Washington while Congress was in session. He was rarely able to get home, and, when he did, there were long lines of people standing at the door waiting to talk with him."

"In reality, our entire economic system was in jeopardy," Dad explained. "Who would negotiate between the free enterprise companies and the labor unions? There needed to be legislation that would give an appropriate and just balance of power between the presidents and owners of companies and the work force. That's where the Taft-Hartley Act came into play.

"Grandpa was a great debater. He could beat anybody in a debate. In live arguments before enormous crowds, he would use the statements of the opposition to win his point. Those who opposed him sounded foolish. He could tongue-tie people faster than anyone and never lose his cool. He had a great sense of humor and was able to use it for his advantage when facing open debates, whether in front of an audience of thousands with open microphones or on the radio. This was back before the days of television. Once his reputation was known, he was asked to be the voice of the Republicans. Every weekend he would do the national radio spot for the Republican Party. This went on for years.

"We have been with Grandpa and have met President Truman and other world leaders, not only in the White House but actually in the Oval Office. Grandpa was a guest of the President almost every week. I was with him in the Oval Office probably a dozen times."

As I listened to all this, I was amazed I had heard none of it before. It was at that moment I learned why in the year 2000 at the turn of the millennium one of the leading national newspapers voted my grandfather one of the fifty most influential people of the past one hundred years. In fact he was one of only two congressmen who were included on the list. Listening to my dad and his brother discussing their dad, I experienced a deep and profound sense of identity, purpose, security, and confidence breathing deep into my own masculine soul. It was as if I were seeing a reflection of myself in the words of their portrait of their dad, my grandfather. My name is identical to his, only he was Junior, and I am the III. Our name, Fred Allan, means "peaceful leader"; the venues of our leadership are different, but our calling and gifting are quite similar.

This past Saturday I had the opportunity to chauffeur my grandmother Hartley to her one hundredth birthday celebration. This forty-five minute drive was one of the most enriching moments in my life. She sang songs, reflected on her life, her marriage, her deep love and admiration for her deceased husband (the congressman), her vibrant relationship with God, and her born-again experience. She even quoted Shakespeare—a few lines from *Othello*. The words marinated in my mind, and when we arrived at the party, I requested that she quote them for everyone, and she was glad to oblige. In replaying the videotape and comparing her performance to my copy of *Othello*, she had it word perfect.

> Good name in man and woman, dear my lord,
> Is the immediate jewel of their souls.
> Who steals my purse steals trash; 'tis something,
>   Nothing;
> 'Twas mine, 'tis his, and has been slave to thousands;
> But he that filches from me my good name
> Robs me of that which not enriches him
> And makes me poor indeed.

I read those words in college English but they never meant so much—not until now. Sitting next to my one-hundred-year-old grandmother, knowing that I turn fifty later this year, listening to her talk about the wealth of a good name, knowing that I bear the name of the man she most admired—I couldn't help but take to heart the message.

Later that evening, after driving her back to her nursing home, wheeling her chair back to her room, saying our final good-byes—knowing how final they may well be—I leaned over, kissed her cheek, and vowed to heed her words and uphold the treasure of a good name.

The message she gave me is the message of this book—the power of passing on a good name. There is no higher calling any of us will ever have.

This is parenting at its best!

Notes

Chapter 1 I Accept You

1. Richard Hoffer, "What Bo Knows Now," *Sports Illustrated,* 30 October 1995, 56.

2. Ibid.

3. Ibid.

4. Ibid.

Chapter 2 I Understand You

1. Quoted in William Manchester, *The Last Lion* (Boston: Little, Brown, 1983), 182–83.

2. Ibid., 209.

Chapter 3 I Honor You

1. Rick Reilly, "The Real Super Bowl Winner," *Sports Illustrated,* 3 February 2001, 108.

2. Ibid.

3. Ibid.

4. Gary Smalley and John Trent, *The Blessing* (Nashville: Thomas Nelson, 1986).

5. Quoted in ibid., 43.

6. Dotson Rader, "A Chance to Go the Distance," *Parade,* 6 July 1997, 4–5.

7. Tracey Stewart, *Payne Stewart: The Authorized Biography* (Nashville: Broadman and Holman, 2000).

8. Smalley and Trent, *The Blessing.*

9. James Dobson, *What Wives Wish Their Husbands Knew about Women* (Wheaton, Ill.: Tyndale, 1975), 157–58.

10. The DISC Personal Profile System (Carlson Learning Co., 1994) can be acquired from Walk Thru the Bible, 4201 N. Peachtree Road, Atlanta, GA 30341, 1-800-868-9300.

11. Franklin Graham, *Rebel with a Cause* (Nashville: Thomas Nelson, 1997), 313.

Chapter 4 I Like You

1. James Collins and Jerry Porras, *Built to Last: Successful Habits of Visionary Companies* (New York: Harper Business, 1994).

2. Archibald Hart, *Adrenaline and Stress* (Dallas: Word, 1995).

Chapter 5 I Love You

1. Gary Chapman, *The Five Love Languages* (Chicago: Northfield, 1992).

2. Quoted in Jay Kesler, *Parents and Teenagers* (Wheaton, Ill.: Victor, 1984), 259.

3. Ibid., 285–86.

4. Jarrett Bell, "Buoniconti Honored as Player, Dad," *USA Today,* 6 August 2001, 8C.

5. C. S. Lewis, *The Four Loves* (New York: Harcourt, Brace, 1960), 68.

Chapter 6 I Love You Anyway

1. Quoted in Kesler, *Parents and Teenagers,* 40.

2. C. S. Lewis, *An Anthology of C. S. Lewis: A Mind Awake,* ed., Clyde S. Kilby (New York: Harcourt, Brace and World, 1968), 73.

3. Alice Smith, *Beyond the Veil* (Ventura, Calif.: Regal, 1997), 117–18.

4. Quoted in John Eldredge, *Wild at Heart* (Nashville: Thomas Nelson, 2001), 32.

Chapter 7 I Protect You

1. See MSNBC.com/news 4.10.02.

2. Gerhard Kittel, *The Theological Dictionary of the NT,* vol. 1 (Grand Rapids: Eerdmans, 1974), 209.

3. W. R. Nicoll, *Expositor's Greek Testament,* vol. 2 (Grand Rapids: Eerdmans, 1960), 722.

Chapter 8   I Am Proud of You

1. Hal Bodley, "Co-MVP Schilling's Dream Comes True," *USA Today,* 5 November 2001, 4C.

2. Erma Bombeck, *Family—The Ties That Bind . . . and Gag!* (New York: Fawcett Crest, 1987), 2–3.

Chapter 10   I Empower You

1. Quoted in personal letter from Jack Hayford, 10 June 2001.

2. Quoted in William McDonald, *True Discipleship* (Kansas City: Waltrick, 1962), 27.

3. Quoted in John Piper, *God's Passion for His Glory* (Wheaton, Ill.: Crossway, 1998), 81.

4. Ibid.

5. Ibid.

Fred A. Hartley III, author of nine books, which have sold half a million copies, is senior pastor of Lilliburn Alliance Church in the metro-Atlanta area. A graduate of Wheaton College and Gordon Conwell Theological Seminary, he is a popular speaker at universities and conferences around the country and worldwide. Fred and his wife, Sherry, have four adult children, who share their side of the story in this book on parenting.

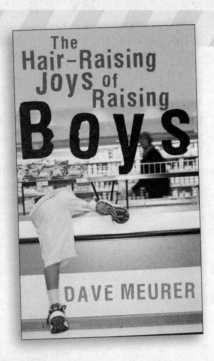

Shape your family with the qualities
that will make it *shine!*

"This down-to-earth book will take your family from good to great!"—**Dr. Kevin Leman,** author of *Making Children Mind without Losing Yours*

MOM-TESTED
MOPS
Mothers of Preschoolers
MOPS-APPROVED

Five Simple Ways to Grow a Great Family

CAROL KUYKENDALL

Build a healthy family that wants to be together, grow together, and stay together—a family that will shine from one generation to the next.

This is the advice you've been looking for!

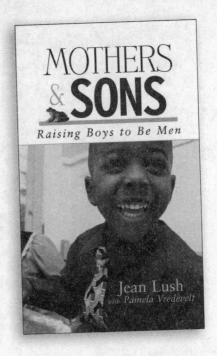

Encouragement and practical insight for raising boys to be men . . . a mother's imprint on her son lasts forever.